ELITE EIGHTH

KENTUCKY'S DOMINATING 2012 CHAMPIONSHIP SEASON

TRIUMPH
BOOKS

Victoria Graff

This book is available in quantity at special discounts for your group or organization.
For further information, contact:

Triumph Books LLC
814 North Franklin Street
Chicago, Illinois 60610
Phone: (312) 337-0747
www.triumphbooks.com

Printed in U.S.A.
ISBN: 978-1-60078-778-2

The Danville Advocate-Messenger and *The Winchester Sun*
Schurz Communications, Inc. and Advocate Communications, Inc
Scott C. Schurz Jr., President, Editor and Publisher
John C. Nelson, Executive Editor
Larry Vaught, Sports Editor, *The Advocate-Messenger*
Keith Taylor, Sports Editor, *The Winchester Sun*
Book Editor: Gary Moyers, Advocate Communications
Photographers: Clay Jackson and Victoria Graff

Content packaged by Mojo Media, Inc.
Joe Funk: Editor
Jason Hinman: Creative Director

Front and back cover photos by AP Images

Getty Images

Contents

Introduction

What Began as a Goal in Preseason Ends in Eighth National Title for Kentucky

By Larry Vaught

Kentucky's year-long national championship quest is over thanks to a 67–59 victory over Kansas in the national championship game.

Not only did Kentucky win 38 games, go unbeaten in regular-season Southeastern Conference play and lose just twice all season — a buzzer-beater at Indiana that led to fans storming the court and a rare final-four-minute scoring collapse against Vanderbilt in the SEC Tournament — but the Wildcats accomplished what every player on the roster planned on since last April.

Sophomores Doron Lamb and Terrence Jones turned down chances to go to the NBA a year ago to be part of a national championship team and loved giving coach John Calipari his first title. "Coach is coach and helped so many people and has changed so many lives. He is a good coach and a good person. If we lose, he tries to take all the blame. If we win, he gives us all the credit. That's why he deserved this more than anybody and I am so glad I came back to be part of giving it to him," Jones said.

Lamb said players openly talked all summer about winning the championship, one reason pressure did not bother the team all season.

"Before the season started, everybody expected us to win every game, and we wanted to really do this," Lamb said. "We had to deal with pressure and expectations all season. We didn't brush that off because we wanted to win the whole thing."

Michael Kidd-Gilchrist—one of three freshmen starting for the Wildcats—shook off an early shoulder injury and delivered 11 points and six rebounds in support of UK's title-game win over KU. (Victoria Graff)

Freshmen Marquis Teague, Michael Kidd-Gilchrist, Anthony Davis and Kyle Wiltjer all started talking about winning a national title — and going undefeated — when they were playing high school all-star games after their high school senior seasons ended.

"It was a great year for us. We have seven starters who all decided from Day One to be unselfish and take this thing as far as we could. We've had a lot of fun," Teague said. "Coach Cal told us whether we won or lost the national title we had a great year, but we wanted a championship. We are all unselfish and we trust each other. We know if we gave somebody the ball in position to make a play, they would make a play. But the biggest thing is we just trusted each other and knew we could do this."

Kentucky's run to the national championship faced four major nonconference tests. The Wildcats beat Kansas 75–65 in the State Farm Champions Classic in New York on Nov. 15 in their second game of the season thanks to a second-half blitz that had all five starters score in double figures. Next came a classic 1-2 matchup with North Carolina in Rupp Arena Dec. 3 that UK won 73–72 thanks to an incredible block by Anthony Davis of John Henson's potential game-winning shot.

That set the stage for the Dec. 10 game in Bloomington, Ind. Davis got in early foul trouble, Teague struggled in the first half and Jones was so poor — four points, one rebound — that Calipari benched him at the end of game. Lamb missed a key free throw late and Indiana won on a 3-point shot by Christian Watford after UK failed to foul as Calipari wanted since the team had a foul to give.

The New Year's Eve game with Louisville in Rupp Arena took Kidd-Gilchrist's best overall game of the year — 24 points, 19 rebounds — for UK to survive 69–62. About three months later, UK beat Louisville 69–61 in the Final Four.

Conference play did one major thing early for Kentucky — it made the Cats more physical. Kentucky had to come from behind to win 65–62 at Tennessee and then hit a different gear after a hard takedown from behind of Davis at LSU inspired the Cats to win 74–50. Kentucky followed that game with a 25-point win over Tennessee, 34-point win over South Carolina and 20-point victory over Florida in its most dominating stretch of the season.

The Cats got a major challenge at Vanderbilt before winning 69–63 on Feb. 11 and 10 days later trailed 41–28 at Mississippi State before a 45–23 second half blitz gave Kentucky a 73–64 victory that again featured five players in double figures — a familiar theme for a team that depended on balanced scoring and the nation's top field goal percentage defense all season.

Kentucky closed the regular season with a 74–59 win at Florida and then was so-so in SEC tourney wins over LSU and Florida before a late scoring drought led to a 71–64 loss to Vanderbilt.

However, the Cats hit another gear in NCAA Tournament play. Kentucky dominated Western Kentucky 81–65 and rolled over Iowa State 87–71. The rematch with Indiana was an offensive shootout the Cats won 102–90 before UK hit Baylor with a first-half knockout to win 82–70. The set the stage for the Battle of the Bluegrass in New Orleans against Louisville that UK won and then the rematch with Kansas that gave UK the national title.

Davis was a consensus choice as national player of the year after leading the nation in blocked shots. Calipari marveled at his team's offensive efficiency.

"All year our goal was to win the championship," said senior Darius Miller, who set a UK record by playing in his 152nd game in the title contest. "We had fun all year and I think we are all just honored to be part of something like this. We thought we could do, but saying it is a lot easier than doing it."

Maybe, but not for Kentucky this year because the team that wanted to win the title did exactly that. ■

Kentucky's stifling defense was key to this season's championship run. Here, Terrence Jones harasses KU player-of-the-year candidate Thomas Robinson during the championship game. (Victoria Graff)

NCAA Tournament Semifinal

Game Date: March 31, 2012

Location: New Orleans, Louisiana

Score: Kentucky 69, Louisville 61

Terrence Jones Shows He Can Impact Kentucky by Doing More than Just Scoring

By Larry Vaught

For almost 34 minutes, Terrence Jones did almost nothing to make sure that the reason he came back to Kentucky for a second season was going to happen.

Jones bypassed going to the NBA after UK lost to Connecticut in the 2011 Final Four because he wanted to win a national title. Yet when Louisville turned a 46–34 deficit into a 49–49 tie with 9 minutes, 12 seconds to play, Jones had been playing like he was auditioning for a part on UK superfan Ashley Judd's TV show, *Missing*.

He wasn't rebounding, as the Cardinals owned the boards in a way no team had this season against UK. He wasn't scoring. His defense was suspect. Kentucky coach John Calipari got so infuriated with Jones that he jerked him out and scolded him harshly on the bench.

"We've got a great relationship," said Jones. "He tells me what he sees. I don't see things playing as well as he does. When he tells me, I do it."

Or at least he did to end the game and that's a major reason UK won 69–61 to advance to the national championship game. Jones finished with six points, seven rebounds, two blocks and two steals. He was only 3-for-8 from the field and 0-for-3 at the foul line.

But he powered his way inside to score with 6:21 left to give the Cats a 55–51 lead. He got a defensive rebound, missed a contested shot and got another defensive rebound that set up a 3-pointer by Darius Miller. He got another rebound and blocked Louisville guard Russ Smith's shot. He drove inside and scored to make it 62–53 with 2:27 left, and the Cats held on to a win in a game that fascinated the state all week.

This was the first Final Four matchup between the rivals, and as much as both teams

Anthony Davis blocks a shot by Louisville's Peyton Siva in the second half. Davis' five blocked shots were a key factor in UK's 61–61 win. (Victoria Graff)

Anthony Davis
(center), winner of
the 2012 Naismith
Trophy, celebrates
as he walks off the
court following
Kentucky's win over
Louisville in the
NCAA Semifinal.
Teammates Doron
Lamb (left) and
Terrence Jones
follow Davis off
the court.
(Victoria Graff)

tried to say it was just another game, it wasn't. A walk down Bourbon Street Friday night confirmed that. A walk anywhere near the Superdome Saturday verified that. The noise level inside the dome confirmed it.

"We're one game closer to our dream and achieving our goal," freshman center Anthony Davis said. "Our fans are great to us. We just go out and play ball, but we want to give them a show and give them what they want, which is a national championship."

Davis played like the consensus national player of the year and was the overall difference in the game. He had 18 points (7-for-8 from the field), 14 rebounds, five blocked shots and two assists. Just his presence allowed other Wildcats to get easy shots — a big reason UK shot 57.1 percent (28-for-49) from the field.

As the game ended, Davis threw the ball high into the air, took out his mouthpiece and said, "This is my stage." It was a rare show of emotion by the UK All-American, but it was that kind of game.

"It was a close game and was very emotional," Davis said. "We fought the whole game. We come to Kentucky built for this. We go hard in practice. We are out there to have fun. I am just glad to be here with a national championship chance as a freshman. I had to do this for my team. I knew I could make plays. My team needs me to play well and that's what we did tonight."

True, but Davis and his teammates need Jones to play like a lottery pick, too. And that's especially true when Michael Kidd-Gilchrist, UK's most physical player, gets in early foul trouble. With Kidd-Gilchrist limited, the Cards banged on Davis to wear him down and dominated the rebounding most of the second half before Jones came alive.

Opposite: Terrence Jones slams home for two of his six points against Louisville. Jones' rebounding and scoring late in the game were crucial as the Wildcats pulled away. Above: Michael Kidd-Gilchrist dunks late in the second half. The freshman scored Kentucky's final six points. (Victoria Graff)

"We knew the game would stay close," Jones said. "Nobody's going to quit in this atmosphere and certainly not Louisville. They got a lot of offensive rebounds and those final minutes I just could not let my team down. Coach told me to get in there and fight and get the ball, so I did."

Sounds simple. So why did it take so long to "get the ball" for Jones?

"I was thinking too much. I was worried about last year [and losing in the Final Four]," Jones said. "Then it was like I saw the time left and knew I had to play a lot better. I don't think it was the pressure of the rivalry or anything. We just finally got the job done like we have all year. They made runs. We made runs. It was just a great win."

For Louisville, it was a difficult loss to a Cinderella Final Four run. However, Louisville coach Rick Pitino said he told Calipari after the game he would be "pulling for you" to win the national title and to "bring the trophy back home to Kentucky."

That trophy hasn't been "brought back home to Kentucky" since 1998. That's a long time for the Wildcat faithful to go without a title and the players know they want one just as much as the team does.

"I am sure the fans will be the same way the next game [Monday]," Miller said. "No matter who we play, we always have great fan support. I am sure they wanted this one bad, but to us it really was just the next game because our main goal is to win a championship, not beat a certain team."

However, beating that "certain team" from the Bluegrass State has UK back in the title game for the first time since 1998 and Kentucky within one game of the national championship quest it has been pursuing all season. ■

Opposite: Michael Kidd-Gilchrist embraces teammate Anthony Davis as the final buzzer sounds. Above: Doron Lamb shoots in the lane against Louisville's Gorgui Dieng. Lamb scored 10 points in the win. (Victoria Graff)

Louisville Coach Rick Pitino and the Cardinal Players Know Anthony Davis Makes the Difference for Kentucky

By Keith Taylor

Louisville coach Rick Pitino knew for his team to beat Kentucky, or even compete with the Wildcats, it had to win the rebounding battle.

"We knew they were going to play like starving dogs on the glass. We haven't eaten in a week, and the only food for us is the rebound. We had a very difficult time early. The game early, when we got behind, really hurt us. It took so much incredible energy to get us back in the game, and they gave it," Pitino said after UK's 69–61 win that put the No. 1 Cats into the national title game.

Louisville won the rebounding battle 40–33 and had 19 offensive rebounds. Still, the Cards shot just 34.8 percent (24-for-69) from the field and Pitino and his players knew why — Kentucky freshman Anthony Davis.

"The difference, quite frankly, is just Anthony Davis, who will be the No.1 player picked in the draft. When you're playing against Bill Russell at the pro level, you realize why the Celtics won 11 world championships. When you see this young man at the collegiate level, you realize why they're so good. Not that their other players aren't, but he's so much of a factor," Pitino said.

Davis had 18 points on 7-for-8 shooting from the field. He had 14 rebounds, including 12 defensive boards, and blocked five shots. The Cardinals couldn't guess how many shots he changed.

"Anthony Davis, he's a great player. He can change every shot. Everything we try to get close into him, he's just so — I would say he has good footwork. He kind of falls back a little bit and times his shot pretty well," Louisville guard Chris Smith said.

"He just has great length, so he's able to alter shots. It's difficult for guards like Peyton [Siva] and Russ [Smith] to get a clean look like they usually do," Louisville teammate Kyle Kuric said.

"Without Anthony Davis, they are average defensively, they are pretty good, but with him, they are No. 1 in the country," Russ Smith said. "At the end we couldn't capitalize on all those chippy shots around the basket. We had so many opportunities, but we couldn't score."

Russ Smith was 4-for-15 from the field. Peyton Siva was 4-for-11 and Chris Smith 3-for-11. Center Gorgui Dieng was just 3-for-10 from the field against Davis.

But Russ Smith said Kentucky's whole demeanor makes the Wildcats difficult to beat.

"They have everyone in attack mode going to the basket all the time, everyone attacks offensively," Smith said. "That's what they're great at. They are always looking to score."

However, Pitino said to beat Kentucky, it starts with figuring out how to evade Davis' defensive presence.

"I think a little bit at the end, you've got to get the shot-blocker. What they do is if you run a pick-and-roll, he stays in the lane. You got to get your people to seal him, bother

Coach John Calipari shouts instructions to his players during Kentucky's win over Louisville. With the win, Calipari advanced to his second career NCAA Championship Game. (Victoria Graff)

him, duck in on him, overpower him," Pitino said. "Gorgui is not at that stage to do that yet."

"Are they beatable? No question about it, because Vanderbilt did it. But you're going to have to play great offense, great defense, and you got to bring you're A-plus game and they have to have a B game. That's what has to happen. They're a great ballclub. You have to get one or two guys in foul trouble. But Kansas and Ohio State are capable of having an A-plus game, and so are we. We just didn't have it."

Pitino's 1995-96 national championship team at Kentucky had a roster full of future NBA players like this UK team does and dominated most teams like the Cats have this year. Still, Pitino said every team is "different" and noted that his 1996 championship team was deeper.

"But their six are every bit as good as our [first] six, so you can't really compare eras," Pitino said. "I will say this, that Anthony Davis is as fine a basketball player as there is. They have a great basketball team, one that I know John [Calipari] is really proud of. To tell you the truth, I haven't always liked some of the Kentucky teams. I'm not going to lie to you. But I really like this team a lot because of their attitude and the way they play.

"I'll certainly be rooting for them hard to bring the trophy back to Kentucky because I'm really impressed with them, not only as basketball players, the way they carry themselves, their attitude. They're a great group of guys, doing a tremendous job. Louisville will be rooting for Kentucky, which doesn't happen very often, to bring home that trophy to the state." ■

NCAA Championship Game

Game Date: April 2, 2012

Location: New Orleans, Louisiana

Score: Kentucky 67, Kansas 59

Kentucky Now Has the Title that the Players Expected to Win All Season

By Larry Vaught

It looked like winning an eighth national championship might be a lot easier for Kentucky than it ended up—a 67–59 victory over Kansas.

Kentucky was magnificent the first half and built a 39–21 lead with 2 minutes, 52 seconds left in the half. However, Kansas not only cut the margin to 41–27 at halftime, but national-player-of-the-year Anthony Davis got his second foul. Still at 59–44 with only 5:13 to play, it looked like Calipari's team could coast to the title.

Wrong. Kansas eventually trimmed the lead to 62–57 with 1:37 left and every UK fan in the Superdome — plus everyone watching on CBS-TV — took a big gulp and worried that this team might let its legacy slip away.

"We never doubted," senior Darius Miller said. "We knew we would be fine."

And they were. Jones hustled to save a turnover that Davis converted into a free throw. Kidd-Gilchrist blocked Tyshawn Taylor's reverse lay-up and Teague made two free throws for a 65–57 lead with 53.9 seconds left and the party was ready to start.

When the final horn finally sounded, there was Jones hugging Kidd-Gilchrist. Davis gave assistant coach Kenny Payne a huge bear hug. Calipari hugged anyone who would let him.

"I am happy for our players and I am happy for our fans. This is a great thing for our school and our state," Calipari said.

As he has all season, Calipari gave the players all the credit. He constantly insisted during the NCAA Tournament that it was about them, not him winning his first national title. That didn't change after this game.

Terrence Jones shows off his reward for returning to Kentucky for his sophomore season: the NCAA Basketball Championship Trophy, earned thanks to UK's 67–59 win over Kansas. (Victoria Graff)

"Coach was happy, but he said it was the players who won the title, not him," senior Eloy Vargas said. "He was not that different than any other game really."

Calipari joked he was ready to go "back to the hotel and go to bed" — something that certainly wasn't going to happy with family, friends and UK fans waiting at the hotel and a massive Rupp Arena celebration planned when the team arrives back home Tuesday to deliver the championship trophy that UK fans live to have.

This game was a perfect example of why Calipari's team was so hard to beat. Kentucky was just 7-for-26 from the field the second half. Davis was just 1-for-10 from the field in the game and didn't score the first half. But it didn't matter. Not on this team of unselfish players who prided themselves on always finding a way to win.

Lamb was spectacular and went over the 1,000-point mark in his career by pouring in 22 points on 7-for-12 shooting. When Kentucky needed a key second-half shot, he hit it. Teague was only 5-for-14 from the field, but had 14 points and three assists.

Jones had just nine points and seven rebounds, but he played as hard and with as much effort for 29 minutes as he has at any time in his career. He blocked two shots, got a steal and helped harass Kansas star Thomas Robinson into going 6-for-17 from the field.

Then there was Davis. How many players can change a game without scoring? Not many. But Davis did with 16 rebounds, five assists, six blocks and three steals. He

Opposite: Anthony Davis struggled to score against Kansas but he was a monster on the defensive end, blocking six shots and grabbing a dozen rebounds (to go with four more offensive boards). Above: Doron Lamb poured in 22 points on 7-of-12 shooting to lead the UK offensive attack. (Victoria Graff)

intimidated the Jayhawks — one big reason Kansas shot just 35.5 percent.

Davis insisted after the game he would not make a decision about his future until sitting down with Calipari and his parents later this month. But he's gone to the NBA where he will be the No. 1 pick after a season where he led UK in scoring, rebounding, blocked shots and steals. He did it all, and never cared about anything but winning.

"It doesn't matter if I don't score. If we win, that's all that counts," Davis said.

"We tried to take it to 'em. We tried to force help. The second half, the shots he blocked, the majority went out of bounds, which is okay," Kansas coach Bill Self said. "He is an unbelievable factor on both ends, but certainly defensively he's got timing, his first jump is unbelievable, and he's a very smart defender as well."

He's also a great teammate and that was a major reason this team was so unselfish and cared so much about each other. Kidd-Gilchrist was the same way. So was Miller. Actually, they were all that way.

That's why they were giddy on the podium receiving the national championship trophy, but a lot happier when they got to go up into the stands to see family members. Jones didn't want to let go off the trophy he came back to Kentucky to win, but he gladly gave it up to go hug his mother, aunt and grandmother. "I couldn't wait to get up there to see them," he said. "They mean everything to me."

Kidd-Gilchrist's mother, Cynthia Richardson, was on the court after the game taking pictures and smiling as

Opposite: KU kept Anthony Davis in check on offense, but Kentucky had too many scoring threats—namely, Lamb, Teague, and Kidd-Gilchrist—for the Jayhawks to shut down. Above: Terrence Jones scored just nine points but his high-intensity play at both of the court was a major factor in the Cats' victory. (Victoria Graff)

she watched her son on the national championship podium.

"This is what we came to Kentucky for. We really believed this could happen, and it did. I am so proud of him," she said.

Calipari didn't show a lot of emotion, but he didn't hide his feelings for this team that had been ranked No. 1 most of the season yet had heard time after time that a team built on one-and-done players that depended on freshmen couldn't win a title. Maybe that had been true, but the Wildcats busted that myth for good with this win.

"Listen, this team deserves all the accolades that they've been getting. And what I wanted them to show today is that we were not just a talented team, we were a defensive team, and we were a team that shared the ball," Calipari said. "I wanted everybody to see it because it became, 'They're more talented than everybody.'

"We were the best team this season. We were the best team. The most efficient team. We shared the ball. I've wanted that. I told them I wanted this to be one for the ages. Go out there and show everyone what kind of team you are, even though we were young. It doesn't matter how young you are, it's how you play together."

And this season no one played together better than Kentucky. ■

Opposite: Kentucky senior and super-sixth-man Darius Miller celebrates bringing the championship trophy back to his home state, a fitting end to a fine four-year career. Above: KU were no slouches on defense, as Anthony Davis—here, being challenged by Jayhawk Jeff Withey—discovered in the title game. (Victoria Graff)

UK Coach John Calipari Predicted Doron Lamb Would Have Great Game and Lamb Delivered

By Keith Taylor

When Kentucky finished its shoot-around Monday at the Superdome, coach John Calipari predicted to his team that sophomore guard Doron Lamb would score 25 points in the national championship game against Kansas.

"He just told us Doron was shooting great and was on fire the whole practice," senior Eloy Vargas said. "Coach said he knew he was going to have a great shooting game. He didn't get 25, but he got 22 and that's not too bad."

Lamb's 22 points in the 67–59 victory over Kansas helped UK win its eighth national title. He was 7-for-12 from the field and 3-for-6 from 3-point range. Kentucky got only seven field goals the second half after building an 18-point lead in the first half, but Lamb had back-to-back 3-pointers in the second half.

"At the shoot-around when I watched him, I said he'd get 30 tonight. I'm a little disappointed he only got 22. I exaggerated, I said 25," Calipari said. "He is as good a guard when his motor is moving as any guard in the country. He can play multiple positions. He shoots it. He makes free throws. He's good with the ball. He's crafty. I knew he'd have a big game. I knew it."

Lamb was hoping Calipari was right.

"I had a great shoot-around. He told me I'd have 25 today, but I had 22. It feels great. My sophomore year, a championship, my second time to the Final Four, can't get no better than that.

"It means a lot to me. I worked hard to get here. Coach Cal told me I'm going to have a big game today. Had a great shoot-around. I made a lot of shots today and helped my team to win."

While Lamb is Kentucky's most prolific shooter, he has had to learn how to drive inside, play better defense and score within Calipari's team system — all things he showcased in the championship game as well as most of the season. He also went over the 1,000-point mark — he has 1,118 career points — with the championship performance.

"I don't care who gets the spotlight really. I just go out there and play hard and try to win game. We won the whole championship, so I'm just happy for my teammates," he said. "I just go play my role and do what I have to do to win games. If I am wide open I will knock it down and make plays for myself and my teammates."

Lamb was smiling and dancing with teammate Marquis

Kentucky sophomore Doron Lamb averaged nearly 14 points per game during the 2011-2012 season, but he stepped up in a huge way during the national title game, leading the Cats to a championship with 22 points. (Victoria Graff)

Teague during the pregame introductions. He was grinning on the national championship podium with teammates after the game.

"We were loose all year. There ain't no pressure on us really. We just had to go out and finish games," Lamb said. "We had to play every game like it was our last game. Kansas was a great team. But there was no pressure on us. We have a great team, great players. If we just played our roles, we were going to win games. We actually thought it was kind of fun to be the favorite and have everybody coming at us."

Lamb said it was hard to explain why this team filled with future NBA first-round draft picks bonded so well from the start.

"I don't know. We all like each other. We hang out off the court and go to movies and stuff. We do a lot of things together. We all have a great friendship, and it shows on the court. We played great as a team. We played great defense, talked and had a lot of fun," Lamb said. "We never have fights or anything like that. We like each other and have a great time with each other and we go on the court and love that. We played great with each other."

Lamb credited Calipari's "family approach" for much of the team's success and attitude.

"After practice, we always go places together. Eat together, movies together. We do everything together. We are always like that. We are always laughing, joking. We are never mad at each other," Lamb said. "On the court we have a great friendship. We run the court together, get back on defense, rebound together and try to win games.

"He is a great coach, great motivator. He gets you to play your best every play of your life. He expects a lot out of you. I know he is hard because he wants me to be great. I work hard and know that if I listen to him, we will win games. I have always been yelled at by coaches even when I was young. I am used to that. It does not affect me or my game if I get yelled at. It doesn't bother me that much because I know he is for me."

Lamb thought of leaving UK after his freshman season for the NBA but like teammate Terrence Jones, came back to UK to win the title he got Monday night. He's refused to speculate on what lies ahead even though he's projected a late first-round draft choice to early second-round pick.

"I just wanted to finish my season with a bang and go out strong. I go out there every game and play like my last. Every time I play a game, I try to go out there and play hard. I've always been that way and there was no reason to change that," Lamb said. "I am not thinking about the NBA. I just wanted to finish my college season and win the whole thing. If the NBA comes, it comes. But I am not going to worry about that.

"We had a great thing going and won a lot of games and had a great season. I don't think any of us worried about anything but this season and that's why we were so successful. It was never about me or anybody else. It was about our team."

That's why Lamb said he never worried even when Kansas made a late run to get within five points of UK.

"We huddled up and at that moment we just wanted to get stops. Told ourselves we got to get stops to win the game. At the end of the game, we got stops. Marquis [Teague] made the big 3, made two foul shots and I made two foul shots and that was the game." ◾

Doron Lamb thought about departing for the NBA after Kentucky's Final Four run in 2011, but the lure of a national title proved irresistible. The sophomore from Queens, New York, achieved his goal and is still projected as a possible first-round draft pick. (AP Images)

Game Date: November 15, 2011
Location: New York, New York
Score: Kentucky 75, Kansas 65

Lamb Believes Cats Made "Good Statement" with Kansas Win

By Larry Vaught

Sophomore guard Doron Lamb boldly predicted that Kentucky wanted to make a "statement" when it played Kansas at New York's Madison Square Garden on national television.

Kentucky won 75–65 after a sluggish start that produced a 28–28 halftime standoff—and UK coach John Calipari admitted he felt lucky the game was tied—before the Cats took control in the second half with superior shooting (16-for-25 from the field).

"I think we made a good statement today," said Lamb. "We played against a top team that was ranked and beat them. We want to let people know we are the best team in the country and win every game."

"They came out the second half and punched us in the mouth and playing catch up to that team is not something you really want to do when you are laboring to score," Kansas coach Bill Self said.

Lamb's offense helped break the game open early in the second half. The New York native admitted he was nervous early playing in front of hometown fans and family before he "settled down and let game come to me and made shots for my team" in the second half.

Lamb was 4-for-8 from the field, including 3-for-5 from 3-point range, had had 17 points, four rebounds and one assist in 34 minutes of play.

Marquis Teague drives to the hoop. The freshman point guard overcame a tough first half and impressed the Madison Square Garden crowd with 12 points. (Victoria Graff)

Coach John Calapari and guard Marquis Teague look on during Kentucky's 75–65 win over Kansas. (Victoria Graff)

"I really thought they played a lot better the second half and made shots. Lamb got them off to a good start," Self said. "Their best offense for a long time was our bad offense. I really think we helped them, but they were also a lot better the second half than the first half."

Part of that was because freshman point guard Marquis Teague had all six of his turnovers the first half. The second half, he was more poised except for the time he sounded off to several Kansas players and got quickly corrected by UK's coach John Calipari.

"I always tell Marquis to control the ball and listen to Coach and let the game come to you and make open shots," Lamb said. "He was a little frustrated. He was a little excited. Trying to go one on one. He settled down and let the game come to him and that made a big difference for us the second half."

Lamb played a key role on UK's Final Four team last season. He knows not to get too excited over this win.

"It's still early in the second. We have to work and learn how to play as a team," Lamb said. "The first half we did not pass that much. The second half we did. It will come together soon. We have a lot of scorers on this team, a lot of weapons."

Still, Calipari says 60 or more teams could beat the Cats.

"We believe him. We take every game serious like it is our last," Lamb said. "We want to try to win every game this year. We have to go out and play harder than the other team, run our offense through and listen to Coach." ◼

Above: Freshman Michael Kidd-Gilchrist finished with 12 points and a team-high nine rebounds. Opposite: Doron Lamb launches one of his three 3-pointers. Playing in front of friends and family, the New York native went 4-for-8 from the field to finish with 17 points in 34 minutes. (Victoria Graff)

25 GUARD

MARQUIS TEAGUE

By Larry Vaught • February 9, 2012

Really there's no reason for anyone to be overly surprised at the progress Kentucky freshman point guard Marquis Teague has made recently.

Maybe he's not John Wall or Brandon Knight, Calipari's two previous point guards at UK. Maybe he's not Derrick Rose or Tyreke Evans, Calipari's last two point guards at Memphis. But the current Marquis Teague is still plenty good enough to have his name being mentioned not only as a possible NBA first-round draft pick in June, but also good enough to position the Cats to win a national title.

Against Florida on Tuesday, he had 12 points on only six shots to go with a career-high 10 assists. Granted, he had five turnovers, but several came when he tried to make the right plays because he's become a pass-first, shoot-second point guard that this Kentucky team needs. He doesn't have to be Knight or Wall for this talented team. He just has to be a floor general who distributes the ball, plays physical defense and scores when the defense dares him.

"I am just leading my team and trying to get everybody involved," said Teague after Tuesday's game. "I have a lot of great players and scorers on my team, so I am just trying to get them the ball where they can score. If I have a shot, then I get my shot. If not, I just pass."

Key words there from Teague were "my team." He now not only believes he's the team leader on the floor, but he's playing that way and that's a huge reason Kentucky has won its last four games by 20 or more points.

"Yeah, I feel like I am the leader of the team and the point guard. I have the ball 85 percent of the time. I have to make the right decisions, talk to everybody and make sure everybody is in the right spot. Hopefully we keep it going like this," Teague said. "We enjoy winning, so if I've got to take less shots for us to win, that's what I'm going to do."

Calipari was beaming Tuesday night when he evaluated Teague's play.

"What about Marquis Teague? Twelve points, 10 assists. He is playing, getting everybody shots. He ended the half Doron [Lamb] 3, Doron 3. He got him those shots. That gave us some breathing room, up 12. He played well," the Kentucky coach said.

He also played shutdown defense on Florida point guard Earven Walker and helped hold him without a field goal in the 78–58 win.

"He had one play where he broke down, kind of stopped on a play, they had a 3 in the corner right in front of our bench. Short of that, he's terrific. You can't dribble around him," Calipari said. "I'll tell you where he's great: in pick-and-roll defense. It's hard to screen him because he is a pit bull."

That "pit bull" determination came in handy against Walker.

Marquis Teague moves the ball down the court against Chattanooga in an early season win. (Clay Jackson)

"I just wanted to contain him. I know he is a quick guard and shoots the outside shot very well. I just wanted to pressure up on him, contain him and keep him in front of me and keep him out of the lane and making plays for others because they have a lot of shooters," Teague said. "It is really hard to guard a smaller guy, especially him because he is very quick and crafty with the ball. It's a tough challenge. Have to move your feet and play hard."

Florida was supposed to be a big test for Kentucky and Teague. The Gators had lost just one Southeastern Conference game and are ranked No. 8. This was going to be the game where UK had to prove it was for real and that the big wins over LSU, Tennessee and South Carolina were more than just lopsided scores against inferior teams.

"I think we made a big statement. We just wanted to come in and showed that we feel like we can beat anybody that we play and that we can beat them be a good amount, so we just came out and played hard," Teague said. "We heard some stuff like we played weaker teams at the beginning of our conference and stuff like that, but we were just waiting for better competition, and when we did we still win."

Can anybody beat the Cats if they shoot that well (52 percent overall, 60 percent from 3-point range)?

"I don't want to say nobody can beat us, but it will be tough, real tough," Teague said.

Same for games Teague gets a double-double.

"It felt good to do that. I just played my tempo and tried to control the game and make the right decisions," Teague said.

Those decisions include not being afraid to credit teammates for what they do. He cited how Anthony Davis' inside presence makes it easy for him to score sometimes.

Marquis Teague dribbles past Chattanooga's Drazen Zlovaric during UK's 87–62 win on December 17. (Clay Jackson)

"He opens the floor for us a lot because they [defenders] know if they commit [to helping on another player], we are going to throw the lob for him to dunk," Teague laughed and said. "Sometimes they have to pick and choose what they want to do, but either way we are going to get the bucket."

Won't it get more difficult Saturday at Vanderbilt? The Commodores will be hosting ESPN GameDay and since they have already lost three SEC games, they must beat Kentucky to have any chance to challenge for the conference title some college basketball analysts thought they could win this season.

Plus, won't critics tend to downplay the Florida win if Kentucky stumbles at Vanderbilt?

"Yeah, we have to follow it up. We know it is real tough to play there and they are a real good team. We have to go there and give 100 percent effort and try to get another win. We know there are doubters, but we don't doubt ourselves," Teague said.

The Teague doubters won't go away, though. Even during Tuesday's big win, CBS Sports analyst Seth Davis posted this on Twitter: "In the end Marquis Teague, as good as he is, will be UK's undoing. Might not be til last two minutes of championship game but..."

Perhaps Davis could be right, but I don't think so. Neither does Davis.

"Marquis is our leader and is doing a great job running our team. He's playing great and that's when we play great," Davis said. "We all trust him and believe in him." ■

Marquis Teague proved to be the missing piece of the Wildcats offense. Developing into a pass-first, shoot-second guard, the freshman solidified the UK attack. (Victoria Graff)

Game Date: December 3, 2011
Location: Lexington, Kentucky
Score: Kentucky 73, North Carolina 72

Kentucky's 73-72 Win Over North Carolina Was One Game that Exceeded the Hype

By Larry Vaught

Often highly anticipated regular-season games don't live up to the pregame hype, especially when a game was as highly touted as this Kentucky–North Carolina game.

But guess what? Saturday's game did—and maybe even exceeded the hype.

Kentucky won 73–72 because of an almost impossible play freshman Anthony Davis made to block John Henson's baseline shot with about seven seconds to play. Then the Tar Heels surprisingly let the Cats hold the ball the rest of the way even though coach Roy Williams was pleading for a foul to stop the clock.

On this day, though, no one could hear Williams or anyone else. Rupp Arena was that loud for a game that showcased future NBA stars as well as perhaps the two teams that could play for the national championship in April in New Orleans.

"Both teams just gutted it out, just gutted it out," said Kentucky coach John Calipari. "This is supposed to be March, not now. I'm exhausted."

Actually, both teams were exhausted several times during the game, too. It was that intense and the action was nonstop. This was a man's game. How tough was it? Kentucky freshman Michael Kidd-Gilchrist popped his shoulder out of place when a North Carolina defender grabbed his arm as he was driving to the basket in the first half. He laid on the floor in pain for several minutes, and popped his own shoulder back in place.

"It took a lot of heart and just will to win," Kidd-Gilchrist, who had a team-high 17 points and 11 rebounds — his first of many double-doubles to come at Kentucky — said.

Terrence Jones slams the ball during the first half. Jones scored 14 points in the win. (Clay Jackson)

The Wildcats defense scrambles for the ball after Terrence Jones blocked a Tar Heel's shot. (Clay Jackson)

"That's all it took. Heart and will."

What about the shoulder?

"It was painful, very painful. It would be for anybody," he said. "I was driving for a shot and the guy just grabbed my arm and it popped. I heard it. But I knew I wasn't going to let that keep me from playing."

Maybe not every player could have survived a dislocated shoulder and still played, but no one wanted out of this game in front of a national audience on CBS-TV.

"Games like this get you ready for March and that's all that matters right now," Henson, who had 10 points, eight rebounds and three blocked shots, said.

Guess what? He's right.

Remember last year when UK lost at North Carolina in the regular season and then eliminated the Tar Heels in the Elite Eight? That early trip to Chapel Hill was a learning lesson for Calipari's Cats just like this road game was for North Carolina. But it was also a great learning lesson for Calipari's young team, too.

Calipari insisted it was because he doesn't watch much TV that he didn't realize how much the game was being hyped until Friday night. When he did, he delivered a late-night message to his team.

"Look, I didn't realize everybody is making this big deal out of this. It's just another game. Let's learn from it. I've been in a ton of these," Calipari said. "You freshmen, just be there for your team. Be good teammates. Leaders, you three seniors, this is your game. You got to run this.

"They were ready to play. Both teams were ready to play. They came out of the gate. No one stopped. That was 40 minutes. Whoever had the ball last was winning. We got the ball last and we won. That's what happens when two good teams do not quit."

And here are things Calipari and his team learned from this game:

- Kentucky can take care of the ball in a pressure game. The Wildcats had just nine turnovers even though freshman point guard Marquis Teague had four.
- 3-point defense has to improve. North Carolina was 11-for-18 from 3-point range and many were wide-open looks.

- Terrence Jones is better than last year. He had 14 points, seven rebounds, three blocks, two steals and one assist in 35 intense minutes. He played and also led.
- Kidd-Gilchrist is a warrior. Need a play, he'll make it or try.
- Senior Darius Miller might not do everything, but when Kentucky needs a play he's still more than capable of making it.
- Freshman Kyle Wiltjer only played five minutes, but he scored on a nifty inside move and helped for a key second-half turnover.
- Eloy Vargas played just six minutes, but he got two rebounds and did not get pushed around inside.
- Sophomore Doron Lamb was money when the Cats needed him the second half with 10 crucial points in a nine-minute span when he went 4-for-4 from the field.
- North Carolina coach Roy Williams was disappointed his team didn't win, especially since it was the Tar Heels' second loss in eight days (they lost their No. 1 ranking that UK inherited due to a loss at UNLV a week ago). However, he also knew this was not just another game.

"They are a very good basketball team; we think we are very good as well. We didn't play nearly this well last Saturday night, UNLV had a lot to do with it, but I cannot fault my team's effort tonight," the North Carolina coach said.

No one could.

"They're one of the best teams in the country. They're well coached. They never gave up," Calipari said of the Tar Heels.

True, but the same thing is also true about Kentucky and that's why with the plethora of talent on the these two teams, even the players know a Final Four showdown could be coming.

"Yeah, we could definitely see them again," Jones said. "They are a great team. I was trying to convince our younger guys not to think this was the end of the world. It's the seventh game of the year. It was not for the national title."

But next time it could be and that's what made this potential preview so much fun. ▪

UK forward Anthony Davis rejects North Carolina's Harrison Barnes in the first half. (Clay Jackson)

20 GUARD

DORON LAMB

By Larry Vaught · February 10, 2012

Doron Lamb says making shots is not as hard as some might think, but even he admits he's on a bit of a hot streak right now.

Lamb is hitting 49.5 percent this season from 3-point range, but in Southeastern Conference play he's at 55.6 (20-for-36) after going 4-for-5 in Tuesday's win over Florida.

"Yeah, I am shooting the ball very well right now and getting a lot of open looks really. I want to keep doing this and getting shots up and working on my game," said Lamb.

He credits teammates for his success because of the way UK's interior players are posting inside to draw defenders into the lane.

"They are doubling Terrence [Jones] and digging at Anthony [Davis]. If they keep doing that, there are a lot of shooters on the team that can make shots," Lamb said.

Yet no one hits outside shots on this Kentucky team like Lamb, who does not worry about missing "because I know I will make the next two even if I do miss."

He's soared into the lottery pick range of the nbadraft.net mock rankings going to Memphis with the 13th selection. Here's what the draft projection said about the UK sophomore: "Lamb's overall skill set is not fully utilized playing on such a loaded team, but would mesh well with the Grizzlies' group of scorers. Lamb has been arguably UK's most consistent performer this season. Every time the team needs a big

basket, it seems that Lamb answers the call. He's a clutch performer, has underrated point guard ability and is an excellent teammate."

Lamb knows, though, Kentucky needs him to hit open shots.

"I am a good shooter and I know if I miss a lot of shots, I will make the next ones. I am not worried about missing any shots. I just worry about knocking them down," he said. "I do expect to make them. Every time I shoot, I know it is going in so I don't really worry about missing.

"If I am wide open, I think 90 percent will go in really. I have to keep shooting at practice and working on my game and keep getting all the shots up that I can, but when I am open I expect to make shots because that is what I am supposed to do."

He could find himself paired against another superb shooter Saturday in Vanderbilt's John Jenkins, a 44.3 percent shooter (89-for-201) from 3-point range. Jenkins led the SEC in scoring last year with an even 20 points per game and is leading the league again this year with the same average.

"He's doing a lot of getting to the basket and that's why he's getting to the free-throw line," Arkansas coach Mike Anderson said of Jenkins. "Vandy as a team is getting to the free-throw line. They have a veteran basketball team and I think they're using him in different ways to get him open."

Sophomore guard Doron Lamb celebrates after hitting a jumper during Kentucky's win over Western Kentucky in the opening round of the NCAA Tournament. (Clay Jackson)

Jenkins has taken 78 free throws in 23 games and made 66. Lamb has shot 93 and made 77 in 25 games.

Vanderbilt coach Kevin Stallings said Jenkins has improved practically every facet of his game.

"His defense is 100 percent better. He's a very dependable defensive player for us now," Stallings said. "John has really given us so much more than he gave us a year ago — leadership, talking, energy. He's not a guy that's just running around out here trying to figure out where his next shot comes from.

"Obviously the thing that stands out to anyone is what a terrific shooter he is. But he's better off the dribble. He's becoming an assists guy. He's really given us so much more than he did a year ago. He's trying to lead the team and play the game the way it should be played."

Lamb certainly respects Jenkins' play.

"He's a very good player, the kind of player you like to play against because you know how good he is," Lamb said. ∎

Above: Doron Lamb (left) celebrates with Anthony Davis toward the end of Kentucky's win over Louisville on December 31. (Clay Jackson) Opposite: Lamb puts up a shot against Indiana during IU's 73–72 win over Kentucky on December 10. Lamb led UK with 19 points. (Victoria Graff)

Game Date: December 10, 2011
Location: Bloomington, Indiana
Score: Kentucky 72, Indiana 73

Is the Big Blue Glass Half Full or Half Empty After the Indiana Loss?

By Larry Vaught

The Big Blue glass is either half full or half empty today depending on your perspective.

Kentucky's No. 1 ranking is history — at least for now — after a 73–72 loss to Indiana. This time freshman Anthony Davis couldn't block the potential game-winning shot, the way he did a week ago when UK beat North Carolina 73–72, as Indiana's Christian Watford buried a 3-pointer at the buzzer.

Kentucky coach John Calipari was not all that downtrodden after the game. Or at least he indicated he wasn't.

"This was a great game," said Calipari after he managed to get off the court with his players as bedlam broke out with raucous IU fans storming the court — and even trampling one student who fell down. "I am proud of my team. We gutted it out."

The Wildcats did — and didn't.

Here is why the Big Blue glass could appear half empty today to the pessimist:

- Preseason All-American Terrence Jones, who is supposed to be UK's best player, was a no-show much like he was in an early season loss at North Carolina last year. He had four points on just 2-for-3 shooting and one rebound. He made six turnovers and was so bad that Calipari finally benched him late in the game and when he did try to put him back in he gave up a drive to the basket.

"Terrence absolutely gave us a zero today," Calipari said.

Darius Miller goes airborne to defend against Indiana's Victor Oladipo. (Victoria Graff)

- Kentucky had a 71–70 lead with 49 seconds left after Marquis Teague scored. The Cats got a stop, but left the ball with freshman Anthony Davis, a 54 percent free throw shooter. He got fouled and missed the free throw. Calipari said his team should have made another pass to get the ball away from Davis.

  Kentucky got another stop and Doron Lamb, the team's best free throw shooter at 79 percent, got fouled. But he missed the first shot before making the second one with 5.6 seconds left. Overall, UK was just 10-for-17 at the foul line, a costly stat in this game.

  "I was confident, but I just missed," Lamb, who had 19 points (5-for-14 shooting) said.

- Kentucky had two fouls to give when Indiana took the ball out of bounds after a timeout with 5.6 seconds left. Calipari told his team to not just foul once, but foul twice before a shot could be taken. Instead, Marquis Teague swiped at Verdell Jones with no foul called. That forced Darius Miller to pick up Jones, who got to the block with no foul, and he threw the ball to Watford.

  "We were supposed to foul before they crossed halfcourt. Nobody fouled and they made a lucky shot," Lamb said. "I have no idea (why UK didn't foul). A mental mistake."

  Actually, it was a huge mental mistake and would have been for a high school team.

  "The whole timeout was about fouling," Calipari said.

  Bad game by the team's supposed best player, poor free throw shooting and huge mental blunder to end the game. Does that sound like a No. 1 team?

  But wait. On the glass could be half full side, consider this:

- Indiana was brilliant. The Hoosiers were 9-for-15 from 3-point range and 14-for-17 at the foul line. The fought Kentucky to a 30–30 standoff on the board and UK had 17 turnovers. Yet Kentucky still overcame a 10-point deficit in the second half behind the play of Teague, Miller and Lamb to have a chance to win.

  "They (Indiana) played exactly like they had to," Calipari admitted. "They played well. They were aggressive. They attacked the ball. They were great. They deserved it."

  But in perhaps the toughest environment UK will face all season and in the team's first road game, the Cats did fight back and show some moxie in the second half.

- Teague, a freshman and Indiana native, was terrible the first half. How bad? He missed three 1-foot open shots. He was 0-for-5 from the field with three turnovers the first half. Calipari didn't even start him the second half.

  But he had 15 points on 6-for-6 shooting the second half and attacked the basket. More importantly, he didn't make a turnover. "I expected Marquis Teague to play the way he did in the first half, but then he came back and he played well," Calipari said.

  And that was impressive in this game.

- Michael Kidd-Gilchrist was an "animal" again. That was Calipari's description of his freshman — and he was right. He went to war in the first half when others were stymied. He finished with 18 points, nine rebounds and a much better effort game than many of his teammates. Calipari said he played like the best player on the team, and in this game he was.

- Kentucky got only 24 minutes out of Anthony Davis due to foul trouble and he blocked just one shot. He got his fourth foul on a 3-point shot that Calipari called a "bogus" call, but he still had nine rebounds and was 3-for-4 from the field, including a 15-footer he hit. He made mistakes, but he didn't back away and he should learn from this.

  Calipari again seemed to be choosing the positive take from losing to an unbeaten team playing in front of a crowd that had students lined up for hours before the game waiting to get inside and jumping over rails about 10 feet high to get onto to the floor when the game ended.

  "We are pretty good. I have a good team," Calipari said. "We can win different ways."

  Win? Kentucky lost, but Calipari liked his team's comeback that much to see how this learning lesson could pay huge dividends later.

  "The guys who broke off plays, I just sat them down," the Kentucky coach said. "Playing on the road you have to grind it out and take what you can in transition. Defensively, you have got to come up with 50-50 balls. We didn't and that gave them the chance to win."

  So is the Big Blue glass half full or half empty today?

  Let Lamb answer.

  "We are going to think about it, but we are not going to forget it. It's only one game. We can still win the whole thing. Still win our conference," he said. "We just have to fight back." ■

Michael Kidd-Gilchrist scored 18 points and hauled down nine rebounds in Kentucky's only regular-season loss. (Victoria Graff)

20 GUARD

DARIUS MILLER

By Larry Vaught · March 13, 2012

He's never been the best player on any of the four teams he's played on at Kentucky. But senior Darius Miller has those who believe he could be No. 1 UK's most valuable player this season going into NCAA Tournament play, despite going scoreless in UK's first two Southeastern Conference Tournament games before bouncing back with 16 points Sunday against Vanderbilt.

"Miller does so much and is so versatile. They use him so many different ways," said Mississippi State coach Rick Stansbury. "He plays two, he plays three, he plays four. He can do it all. He doesn't care about attention, and that is so rare today. He is the kind of guy you have to have. He's one of those pieces and role player guys who just does whatever a coach wants and does it very, very well no matter what it is. He could be their most valuable player for all he does and what he does to keep the team together. They are good, but Miller makes them better because there's nothing he won't do to help a team win and that's contagious for younger players to see."

Kentucky coach John Calipari appreciates what the former Kentucky Mr. Basketball from Mason County has done, too. He's accepted a role coming off the bench as a senior after starting 69 games the previous two seasons. He's

also grown into a role as a team leader despite his normally mild demeanor on and off the court.

"He's a wonderful young man. There is no question about that. I'm just really proud of the strides he has taken as far as being assertive as a leader," Calipari said. "It's hard. You tell someone to lead, it's hard you have to almost coach them through it. Teaching guys to lead is part of what we are supposed to do as coaches, because if you think they know how to lead they don't; they know how to lead for themselves but not lead a team. He's done it in a quiet way. Aside from that, I'm proud of what he has become as a basketball player."

Miller and the Wildcats open NCAA Tournament play Thursday night in Louisville against either Western Kentucky or Mississippi Valley State. The Wildcats reached the Elite Eight in 2010 before losing to West Virginia and fell to Connecticut in the Final Four in 2011. That was quite a turnaround from Miller's freshman season under then coach Billy Gillispie when UK collapsed, did not qualify for the NCAA and lost at Notre Dame in the NIT.

"My freshman year was kind of rough going to the NIT. We were kind of disappointed with how we finished, but the past couple of years I have had great teams and great

Darius Miller drives past a South Carolina defender during UK's 79–64 win over South Carolina on January 7. (Clay Jackson)

teammates," Miller said. "I never planned on leaving or anything like that. I always planned to graduate from here, but the first year was tough at times. I think it was rough for everybody on the team, but we stuck with it and ended up great.

"All of us that were here were worried about what would happen when coach Cal got here. I am happy he chose me to stay. I have learned a lot from him. I have been here a while. I don't know if I could narrow it down to one thing. I think I have grown up a lot. I feel like I am a way better player than I was. I am a way better person than I was. I think I have just grown up and matured."

Miller, the SEC tourney MVP last season, impressed Calipari immediately with his "feel for the game" and athleticism.

"He had that middle game, he could shoot the ball a little bit, he was a good handler. I knew he had to get in shape and do all those kind of things. The way I coach and the way he plays, the only thing I had to get out of him was the eye of the tiger, a little bit of viciousness, an aggressive intensity which has been a process, that doesn't happen overnight," Calipari said.

But it has happened. Calipari insists Miller will play in the NBA and he certainly has been at his best in clutch situations for Kentucky this season, one reason Miller has not minded the role of sixth man in his senior season.

"I have the same opportunities as everybody else has. We are all focused on one thing and that is winning a national championship no matter what the roles are," Miller said. "My freshman year to my sophomore year was opposites almost. I am just happy we changed so fast. We went from NIT to chance at a championship in less than a year. I feel like we have a pretty good chance this year. We are doing special things and hope that continues. I have been here for a while and have a lot of good memories and met a lot of good people, but there would be no better way to end this than by winning a national championship."

Miller was bitterly disappointed that Kentucky did not win the SEC Tournament. He failed to score in the first two games, but insisted "not to read too much into it" after the second game. He came back in the title game loss against Vanderbilt to start after freshman Michael Kidd-Gilchrist made that suggestion to Calipari and had 16 points, four assists, three rebounds, two assists and one blocked shot.

He's averaging 9.6 points and 2.6 rebounds per game going into NCAA play for the final time. He's shooting 46 percent overall from the field, including 36.8 percent from 3-point range. He has 73 assists and 29 steals. For his career, Miller has scored 1,178 points, grabbed 465 rebounds and handed out 269 assists in his career. He's made 110 steals while playing over 3,600 minutes.

He's also had 40 different teammates during his four years at Kentucky.

"It has been fun experience. I have played with a lot of great players, and talk to everybody to this day. I can say I am blessed to be part of this for four years," he said.

He never let lofty expectations many had for him overwhelm him when he did not meet standards others had for him.

"I have improved as a player. I know that," Miller said. "When that was going on, I really didn't pay attention to outside sources. Coach Cal has preached to stay in the family. My teammates and coaches always been there in good times and bad times. I never paid attention to that.

"I have dreamed about the NBA since I was a little kid. I feel I will have the opportunity to go there. If not, I feel like there are other things I can do. We'll see. But what I want more than anything is to win this national championship. We all do. That's what this team has been about all year and will continue to be about. We can't let a loss [to Vanderbilt] change our dream or goal. We've had one goal since the season started and that has not changed." ■

Darius Miller throws down a powerful dunk during Kentucky's win over Ole Miss on February 18. (Clay Jackson)

Game Date: December 31, 2011

Location: Lexington, Kentucky

Score: Kentucky 69, Louisville 62

Anthony Davis Had the Final Say Against Louisville

By Keith Taylor

Anthony Davis didn't have much of a say in Kentucky's first-half performance against Louisville at Rupp Arena. He did have a lot to do with the final outcome.

The freshman center played just seven minutes in the first half after picking up two fouls in a showdown against the fourth-ranked Cardinals. He didn't attempt a field goal, pulled down four rebounds and blocked one shot.

That all changed in the final 20 minutes.

Davis scored 18 points, blocked five shots and made 12 free throws on 13 attempts in the second half to help lead the third-ranked Wildcats to a 69–62 triumph over Louisville. Despite playing just 27 total minutes, Davis just missed a triple-double with 18 points, 10 rebounds and six blocks.

Davis made it nearly impossible for Louisville to get off a basket in the post, especially in the second frame. The Cardinals, who made most their baskets on drives to the basket in the first half with the 6-foot-10 Davis out of the lineup, couldn't find any alternative ways to score with his length in the post.

"What you have to do to get to the basket against that guy is almost impossible," said Louisville guard Russ Smith who led all scorers with 30 points. "The amount of room he covers around the basket is incredible."

Watching instead of participating wasn't easy for Davis. Who admitted that he was "out of rhythm" after viewing most of the first half from the sidelines.

Marquis Teague challenges Louisville's Tim Henderson. The freshman point guard had only five points and five assists in 29 minutes. (Clay Jackson)

Michael Kidd-Gilchrist skies over two Louisville defenders. The freshman forward led Kentucky with 24 points and added 19 rebounds. (Clay Jackson)

"It was really hard for me to get it going," he said.

Darius Miller said Davis wasn't happy watching the Cardinals dwindle a double-digit lead to 36–33 at the break after the Cats had built a 15-point advantage at the five-minute mark of the first half.

"I know it was tough for him," Miller said. "I know he wanted to be on the court playing, because he knew he could help us."

Davis made sure foul woes didn't become an issue in the final half and "got loose" during halftime by taking as many shots as possible during the team's warm-up period before the second half began.

"Coach [John Calipari] just told me to go out, play aggressive and play like he knows I can play," he said. "That's what I tried to do in the second half. You have to stay strong and play tough."

Although he finally got into the flow of the game late, Davis compared the atmosphere to the Indiana game on Dec. 10 in Bloomington. A total of 52 fouls were called between the two teams, creating a frenzy at the free-throw line.

"It seems like every second a play stopped," he said.

Despite the overabundance of fouls, Davis noticed the electricity in the stands, especially after the Cats began to create spacing between the two foes in the final 20 minutes.

"The crowd was crazy because of the rivalry," he said. "We were out there having fun."

Miller liked having Davis on the court during the final stretch and added that his presence under the basket resulted in a soothing feeling.

"When he's down there, he intimidates people," Miller said. "He changes their shots, blocks their shots and blocks their shots. It's tough to play against somebody like that. He does a great job of helping us on the defensive end."

Not only did Davis alter Louisville's offensive production in the second half, he made 12 free throws that prevented the Cardinals from mounting a serious threat. Davis made four charity tosses during a 7–0 spurt by the Wildcats after Louisville tied the score at 40–40 with 15 minutes remaining.

Taking extra strokes behind the scenes at the free-throw line prepared Davis for what transpired against the Cards. He wasn't perfect, but close enough.

"You just have to keep practicing," he said. "Practice makes perfect." ■

Opposite: Darius Miller drives to the basket. Above: Anthony Davis goes up for a rebound. Davis totaled 10 rebounds in the Wildcats' 69–62 win over their in-state rival. (Clay Jackson)

3
FORWARD

TERRENCE JONES

By Larry Vaught · March 18, 2012

He came to Kentucky hoping to eventually be an NBA lottery pick, and stayed at Kentucky for a second season with a goal of being the No. 1 player in the 2012 draft.

Yet one thing matters even more to sophomore Terrence Jones — winning a national championship — and that's why he didn't mind playing the role of defense first, score whenever Saturday night.

"He's got an all-around game and he told us before the game he was not going to be scoring that much because they were going to double down on him and he was going to do what he had to do to help us win and that was play defense and rebound," said Kentucky guard Doron Lamb after Jones did just that in UK's 87–71 victory over Iowa State on Saturday night.

Jones drew the one-on-one matchup with Iowa State star Royce White, a versatile player who led the Cyclones in almost every statistical category, and had both the power and finesse to score. White had 23 points, nine rebounds, four assists and three steals before fouling out. But during UK's crucial 20–2 run after the game was tied 42–42, he became a non-factor. In fact, Jones held him scoreless for almost 11 minutes in the second half while the Wildcats nailed down a trip to the South Regional semifinals Friday in Atlanta and a date with Indiana, the team that gave them their first loss this season.

"I've known Terrence since high school. He's a year younger than me, but he's always been a good player even coming up through high school. It was fun between me and him," White said. "Obviously, he did enough for them to get the win. I didn't do enough."

Jones had eight points and was only 3-for-9 from the field. Iowa State did normally double team him inside, but he took advantage of that to dish out three assists. But he also got 11 rebounds, blocked two shots and made one steal. He wasn't perfect, but he was more than good enough to allow UK's other players to stay with Iowa State's perimeter players and limit the Cyclones to 3-for-22 shooting from 3-point range.

"Going into the game, the game plan was to make sure the other guys didn't get a lot of points," Jones said. "If he could beat us by himself, then we'd do that. Pretty much when it came down, when we needed a point and it was real close, I just wanted to get a couple stops just so we could spread apart. Once we got it going with a lot of transitional 3's and Marquis [Teague] getting a lot of layups, then we just spread it out."

Kentucky coach John Calipari had a lot of things to like about his team's play.

Darius Miller was sensational with 19 points, six rebounds and three assists. He was 7-for-11 from the field and hit dagger after dagger. He got so emotional in the

Terrence Jones celebrates during the second half of Kentucky's December 31 win over Louisville. (Clay Jackson)

second half he even stopped at midcourt on a timeout and pounded his chest, something Kentucky players have not done this season.

Marquis Teague? Simply his best game of the year. It wasn't just his career-high 24 points or 10-for-14 shooting. It was his seven assists, the pace he kept the team playing. He had just two turnovers, none in the first half, and also played solid defense on Iowa State sharpshooter Scott Christopherson (1-for-4 on 3's). Anthony Davis had his normal double-double — 15 points, 12 rebounds — along with two blocks. Michael Kidd-Gilchrist struggled on offense — 1-for-4 shooting for two points — but he had seven rebounds and helped shut down Chris Allen (16 points on 6-for-19 shooting).

"I said that's about as good as we can play. We played good. I've got a good basketball team. You won't believe this. I've got good players, too. But they're a good team. They're efficient. They play defense. They play hard. They are skilled. They're all skilled. I just got to keep them in the right frame of mind," Calipari said. "I want them to have fun playing. I want to keep challenging them. I want them to just look at this and be happy but not satisfied. Let's just keep stepping."

Jones was not doing any high stepping. Instead, he was making sure his younger teammates didn't get rattled when Iowa State turned a 38–27 halftime deficit into a 42–42 tie with 16:28 left, or when UK had just a 48–44 lead with 14 minutes left when Lamb got his fourth foul.

"We take pride in our defense. We feel if a team is coming back on us it's because we're not doing something right on that end of the court, not because of the offensive end," Jones said. "So we just pretty much said we need to get a couple stops, and that's just pretty much what we did is just lock down and get more stops." ■

Terrence Jones fights Alabama's Nick Jacobs for the ball during the Wildcats' 77–71 win over the Crimson Tide on January 21. (Clay Jackson)

Game Date: February 11, 2012
Location: Nashville, Tennessee
Score: Kentucky 69, Vanderbilt 63

Wildcats Learning to "Relish" Road Wins Like Calapari Wants Them to

By Larry Vaught

Forget that ESPN GameDay had former Notre Dame coach Digger Phelps warning Kentucky fans to be nice and not ruin Vanderbilt's moment in the spotlight. Forget that Vanderbilt was the only team left with a realistic chance to challenge Kentucky for the Southeastern Conference championship. Forget that Kentucky had been on such a tear — winning its last four games by 103 points — that a letdown surely had to be coming.

None of that mattered to coach John Calipari's team at Vanderbilt Saturday night when the Wildcats did something they have not had to do yet this year — come from behind late on the road against a good, experienced team to win.

"Every game we play is like walking into this. We get the other team's best shot and after the game, there are 25 [TV] cameras. Any of the places we have been end up being like this," said Calipari after UK's 69–63 comeback victory. "We handled this game like we have other and will handle future games the same way. On our board, I tell the team to love the road, love this, relish this. Keep in mind, when you are 40 you will think about playing this game."

Michael Kidd-Gilchrist puts up a shot against a tough Vanderbilt defense. Kidd-Gilchrist was limited to just four field-goal attempts. (Victoria Graff)

73

Kentucky players (from left) Anthony Davis, Marquis Teague, and Terrence Jones celebrate during UK's road win over Vanderbilt in Nashville. (Victoria Graff)

They did "relish" the experience.

Perhaps that's why Calipari was almost giddy after the game. Sure, he wished Michael Kidd-Gilchrist had played a little better or Darius Miller had stayed out of foul trouble or Terrence Jones had kept scoring the second half like he did the first half. But Calipari was like a proud papa knowing that his babies had grown into young men after the Cats beat an older, more experienced team that was on fire for the first eight minutes of the second half in front of a crowd ready to celebrate a win. "A lot of people had this as an 'L' for us," Calipari said. "Half of the talking [media] heads said this was the one we were going to get dinged. I don't know if that was their hope or their opinion."

He was joking — I think.

The Commodores weren't laughing, though. Not after this bitter loss when they used a 25–12 blitz to wipe out UK's 13-point halftime lead only to succumb to UK's numbing defense the final 10 minutes.

"Congratulations to [Kentucky]. They made a few more plays than we did. It was a pretty good college basketball game if you didn't care who won. We fought hard. We rebounded hard. They just made a couple more plays than we did. We're very disappointed," Vanderbilt coach Kevin Stallings said. "They're a really good team. They're hard to play against. They had to play tonight to win."

Kentucky did — and it may have taken the heart out of Vanderbilt like apparently the Cats did last week when they beat Florida and then the Gators turned around and lost at home to Tennessee Saturday.

"I feel bad for the fans. The fans always come out and support us. There were people that were out at 5 in the morning and I feel bad for them. I feel like we let our fans down tonight," Vanderbilt senior Jeffery Taylor said. "Obviously, it was a great opportunity for us to come out and get a signature win, it is the last time I get to play Kentucky at home. And losing the game, I think we're all competitors here and I feel like we felt like we had this game."

"I think we played well for the first nine minutes of the game. Then there was an eight- or nine-minute stretch in the middle of the first half where we couldn't score and we couldn't get a stop either. It's tough to come back from that kind of deficit, especially playing the No. 1 team in the country."

Kentucky didn't let the Commodores score the final 4 minutes, 10 seconds, something that seemed unimaginable after Vandy opened the second half 10-for-14 from the field.

"I thought for most part we got pretty good shots in the last four minutes. They made some great defensive plays, some blocks here and there, being in the right place. For the most part we executed what Coach told us to do and they just made some plays," Vanderbilt senior guard Brad Tinsley said.

He's right.

Vanderbilt didn't fold as much as Kentucky just held together and won, something that separates national title contenders from pretenders in March.

"We need all of this. In every huddle, I kept saying this is great for us. It is what we need," Calipari said after Saturday's win. "To be honest, I would rather we be up 23 points. They are an execution team, a veteran team, seniors. They played like that. We got better today.

"This was a good game. They put us in pick-and-rolls. They are an execution team. They are veterans. Our young guys hung around and made plays. We got stronger and tougher. We did a lot of good stuff down the stretch."

They did, but what Kentucky did best was maintain its poise when it could have cracked. Last season's Final Four team did enough to go 2–6 in SEC road play. The Elite Eight team two years lost two SEC road games.

"We knew they were going to make a run. Their gym, they play great here. I never thought they were out of it. We just tried to keep the lead," freshman point guard Marquis Teague said. "We just learned how much heart we all have. We came together defensively. We didn't give up open shots. We just had to fight. We had been beating teams 10 or 20 points, but we knew we could win this."

Believing and doing. Quite a combination when you add this team's talent and why the Cats once again added to their win streak Saturday. ■

Anthony Davis puts up a shot against Vanderbilt. Davis scored 15 points and added eight rebounds in the win. (Victoria Graff)

14 FORWARD

MICHAEL KIDD-GILCHRIST

By Larry Vaught · December 31, 2011

Maybe Michael Kidd-Gilchrist won't be the best NBA player on this Kentucky team, but he's certainly going to be the best player on John Calipari's team this year.

The energetic freshman had 24 points, 19 rebounds and one assist to help lift No. 3 Kentucky to a 69–62 win over Louisville that turned out to be a lot harder than it looked like it might be when the Cats built a 15-point lead in the first half.

In a game that featured 52 fouls and 70 free throws, Kidd-Gilchrist was the one constant. He almost willed Kentucky to victory with his physical effort and relentless play. If he ever takes a play off, it will be his first on either end of the court.

"This is me right here. This is what I live for right here. I've always been that way. I got a lot of heart," Kidd-Gilchrist, who has quickly become a Kentucky fan favorite, said.

It's not any one thing that Kidd-Gilchrist does that overwhelms you. It's just that he does a little bit of everything well.

Center Anthony Davis, the potential No. 1 pick in the 2012 draft, can be dominating and had 18 points, 10 rebounds, six blocked shots and three steals in only 27 minutes (he sat out 12 minutes in the first half with two fouls). But Davis says Kidd-Gilchrist's numbers were no surprise to him.

"He could do that any game. He goes so hard and plays so hard. I don't think anything he does would surprise me," Davis said.

Put sophomore teammate Terrence Jones in the same category after seeing Kidd-Gilchrist set a career-high for points and grab more rebounds against the Cardinals than any other Kentucky player ever has.

"He is an energy player and a game like this really gets him excited," Kidd-Gilchrist said. "He makes all the loose ball and hustle plays. He gets the majority of those plays no matter who we are playing."

There was one time in the first half when Kidd-Gilchrist seemed to go airborne for five feet and land on his belly trying to save a loose ball. He must have hit the deck at least

Michael Kidd-Gilchrist shoots over South Carolina's Malik Cooke during the Wildcats' January 7 win over the Gamecocks. (Clay Jackson)

10 other times in the game. He went to the foul line 13 times, and may have deserved to have been there even more even though you won't ever catch him complaining because the rougher and tougher the game is, the more he likes it.

"I was just feeling it today. I just played good, or think I did," Kidd-Gilchrist said.

Calipari certainly thought he did. He said his star freshman was once again "vicious" on the court and really "stepped on the gas" when Kentucky needed it most.

"He wasn't bothered as much as some of other players by the physical play. He almost relished it," Calipari said.

Forget almost. He loved it.

"This is what I live for," Kidd-Gilchrist, who has scored in double figures seven straight games, said. "I've always been that way. I've got a lot of heart."

Yet that big heart was breaking just a few days ago when his mother was hospitalized back in New Jersey. He almost went home before UK's win over Lamar Dec. 22 to be with his mother a day early. He only stayed and played because teammates asked him to wait.

She was at Saturday's game along with family members and friends. Kidd-Gilchrist had to check his emotion when asked about her after the game and even admitted she had helped teach him "everything" about basketball as well as life.

"It meant a lot [to have her here]. I stayed at the hospital with her. It's very hard to see your mother lying there in a hospital bed and you can't help her," he said. "I was crying my eyes out, but she was able to fight through it."

Maybe that's where he gets the tenacity that helps him fight through anything opponents throw his way — and Louisville did plenty to try and slow him down with little success. He carried the Cats offensively in the first half when

Michael Kidd-Gilchrist shows his enthusiasm on the bench during Kentucky's win over Alabama on January 21. (Victoria Graff)

he had 16 points and his four field goals were as many as the rest of the team had.

But don't think playing basketball gives him an escape from worrying about his mother.

"The game is not an escape," he said. "That's my mother. There's no escape from that. That's real life, not a game."

For Kentucky fans, this game meant almost as much and Kidd-Gilchrist delivered. Maybe it's no coincidence that in UK's other marquee game against North Carolina, he had his only other double-double. Great players tend to play their best on the big stage and there was a reason Kidd-Gilchrist was considered the No. 1 player in his recruiting class for two years before Davis and a few others moved ahead of him in the final recruiting rankings.

But if there is a better all-around freshman in the country, I want to see him.

The Bluegrass Sports Commission named the most valuable player in what had to be the easiest call of the day. "We are proud to present this award to Michael Kidd-Gilchrist," BSC executive director Terry Johnson. "In a very intense rivalry game, Michael stood out with an incredible all-around effort."

But for him, it was just routine.

"This is what I do," he said. "I just play and love playing. The bigger the game, the more I love it because I want to win so bad." ∎

Michael Kidd-Gilchrist and Doron Lamb look on from the bench during the Cats' win over the Crimson Tide at Rupp Arena. (Victoria Graff)

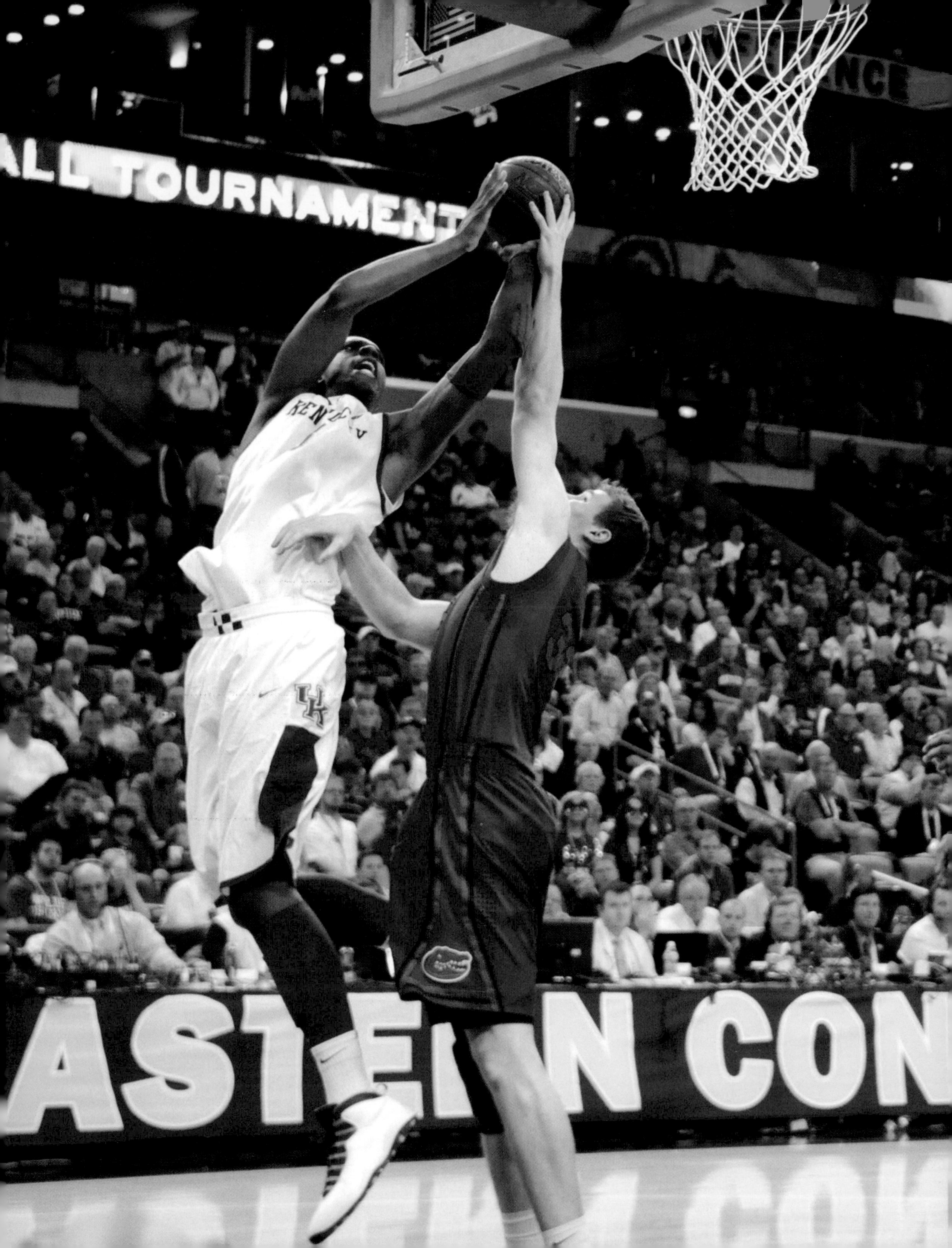
ALL TOURNAMENT
UK

Game Date: March 4, 2012
Location: Gainesville, Florida
Score: Kentucky 74, Florida 59

Terrence Jones, Anthony Davis Help Keep Cats Winning

By Larry Vaught

John Calipari admitted that Kentucky's 15-point win at Florida Sunday was about as well as his team could play.

"If Terrence [Jones] plays like that, we are going to be real good. He competed," Calipari said on his postgame radio show following the 74–59 win. "We are making him block shots [in practice] and not expecting Anthony [Davis] to go get them."

Jones did play "real good", including getting on the floor for loose balls, blocking shots and going inside with authority.

Jones was 9-for-13 from the field and had 19 points, four rebounds, three blocks, two steals and one assist. He had 14 first-half points, the seventh time this season he's going for double digits in the first half. He hit his first 3-pointer since Jan. 21 and had his best scoring game since Jan. 28. He now has 953 points and could reach the 1,000-point mark during the SEC tourney.

"Our point guard again was really outstanding. We only had six turnovers, which means he is really controlling our team," Calipari said of Marquis Teague, who had 12 points and four assists. "Only six as a team is ridiculous."

"Darius [Miller] made shots. Doron [Lamb] made shots. Kyle [Wiltjer] was very good." He's right.

Michael Kidd-Gilchrist was just Michael Kidd-Gilchrist. He was not an offensive force, but his rebounding and defense were as solid as ever.

Then there was Davis, who could be as good as any player ever to play at Kentucky. He hit a 3-pointer. He drove from the 3-point line to score inside. He blocked a shot, grabbed the ball, led the fast break and then followed Kidd-Gilchrist's miss. He hit a right-handed

Terrence Jones drives to the basket during the Wildcats' 74–59 victory over Florida in UK's regular-season finale. Jones scored 19 points in the win. (Clay Jackson)

hook. He hit a left-handed hook. How anyone could not think he's the national player of the year is beyond me.

Davis had 22 points (9-for-13 shooting), 12 rebounds, six blocks and one steal. It was his 14th double-double, second most ever by a UK freshman, and now has 146 career blocks, eighth on UK's all-time list and fifth on the NCAA freshman blocks list. He also hit a 3-pointer for the second straight game and now has scored in double figures in nine of the last 10 games.

"He just scored baskets, was strong with the ball, came up with rebounds. He was really good," Calipari said even though he also thought Florida center Patrick Young was "the best he had seen him" in the game. Didn't matter. Davis was better.

Calipari even joked that ESPN is helping Kentucky by continuing to show over and over Indiana's Christan Watford's winning 3-point shot that gave UK its only loss. Since then, Kentucky has won 22 straight games, including all 16 in SEC play.

"They are playing to win every game. There is no one here playing not to lose," Calipari said. "I keep reminding them of that. Play to win. I am going to take the blame if we lose. I am happy, but not satisfied. We are on a gradual climb. Let's just keep getting better."

Kentucky's players care only about one thing — winning.

They don't believe in that theory that they have won so many games in a row that a loss before the NCAA Tournament would help (sorry Cameron Mills, who noted Sunday morning on a radio pregame show that a loss might refocus the team). They don't worry about who scores (just ask Davis if he's concerned about the player of the year voting). They don't care about records (here's guessing they don't know they became the first UK team to record 30 regular-season wins).

No, they just win. And win. And win.

Some tried to argue Florida had more to gain (Senior Day, SEC Tournament seeding, NCAA Tournament résumé) in this game. But the Cats got off to a great start thanks to the inspired play of Terrence Jones, built a 16-point lead and then took a big haymaker from Florida when the Gators went on a 22–8 run to cut the lead to 46–44.

However, Kentucky did what great teams do. On the road in an arena going crazy in hopes of an upset of the nation's No. 1 team, the Cats went back to work and pulled away to win in impressive fashion.

The NCAA Tournament selection committee has no hopes now of not giving UK the No. 1 seed in the South Region and letting Kentucky start tourney play in Louisville and then go to Atlanta. And I am betting you will see Duke as a No. 2 or No. 3 seed in the South to set up a potential South Region final in prime time 20 years after that historic game in Philadelphia that UK fans will never forget for the wrong reasons.

And what about the defense?

UK shot 53 percent (31-for-59) and is now 44–1 under Calipari when shooting better than 50 percent from the field. But Kentucky also limited the Gators to 21-for-55 shooting, a 38 percent mark. That's the 19th time this season in 31 games that UK has held an opponent under 40 percent shooting. Florida was also 6-for-22 from 3-point range, not much better than its 6-for-27 in an earlier loss at Rupp Arena. Kentucky also had the nine blocked shots and seven steals.

Kentucky came into the game ranked first in the SEC in scoring defense (58.2 points per game) and field-goal percentage defense (38.7). In the final nine minutes, Florida was 1-for-14 from the field.

Remember earlier this season when Vanderbilt went 0-for-9 in the final four minutes to let UK rally to win. Or the defense the Cats put on Mississippi State to overcome a 13-point halftime deficit on the road.

Florida coach Billy Donovan had no complaints about the shots his team took. "About as good as you're going to get against them," Donovan said after the game.

Kentucky plays again Friday at 1 p.m. in New Orleans against the LSU-Arkansas winner and then could get Florida in the semifinals, a matchup the Gators certainly will not want because this Kentucky team just wants to keep doing one thing — winning. ■

Anthony Davis had a game-high 22 points and 12 rebounds in Kentucky's win over Florida. (Clay Jackson)

23 FORWARD

ANTHONY DAVIS

By Larry Vaught • March 20, 2012

Anthony Davis came to Kentucky with big expectations — and may have exceeded them. He openly talked about wanting to win a national championship, something No. 1 Kentucky certainly is in position to do going into the NCAA Tournament. However, he's also leading the nation in blocked shots (166) and is the nation's third best field goal percentage shooter (63.6 percent). He's averaging 14.3 points and 10.1 rebounds per game, both team highs, going into Friday's 9:45 p.m. NCAA Tournament South Region semifinal against Indiana. In 30 of 36 games, he has scored in double figures with 18 double-doubles, the second best total ever by a UK freshman.

The U.S. Basketball Writers Association (USBWA) named Davis its national player of the year Monday after naming him the national freshman of the year last week. He's the first UK player ever to win the ward. He was also named a finalist Monday for Naismith Trophy for college player of the year by the Atlanta Tipoff Club. The other three finalists for the award are Kansas junior Thomas Robinson, Michigan State senior Draymond Green and Creighton sophomore Doug McDermott.

Additionally, he's considered a consensus top pick in the June NBA draft.

"I don't think anybody really knew for sure what kind of player he was," UK radio network analyst Mike Pratt, a former Kentucky standout, said. "We heard about him and heard he could block shots. Because of that, he may have exceeded expectations. John Wall exceeded mine. I just didn't know how quick he was. Big Cuz [DeMarcus Cousins] was as good as advertised.

"I don't believe any scouting services when they rate players. Do you think they watch lateral quickness? They take what college coaches tell them and just plug it into their reports. I think when I looked at him, I didn't think he could be the factor he has been this year. He really knows how to play skilled. When I first saw him, I knew he could play the game. But I didn't know he could take the hits to the body and play. He really knows how to get it done."

Many did wonder if Davis' slim build would negate his shot-blocking skills against heavier, stronger opponents. However, opponents have tried to attack him — or avoid him — in different ways with no real success this season.

"He still has a long way to go to be where I thought he would be offensively, but he's doing more all the time," Pratt said.

Davis has shown his outside shot more and more the last

Anthony Davis slams home two during the second half of UK's win over Western Kentucky in the opening round of the NCAA Tournament. (Clay Jackson)

Anthony Davis finishes a dunk during Kentucky's January 17 win over Arkansas. (Clay Jackson)

month and has also added a left-handed jump hook to his right-handed hook. He's also put the ball on the floor more to drive to the basket the last month.

Still, what he does best is rebound and block shots.

"I never thought he could rebound and block shots and not foul and keep the ball in play the way he has. He does two things — not foul and keep the ball in play better than I ever anticipated," Pratt said. "This kid just knows what he is doing. I just never thought there was any way a kid 18 that had grown so fast would have that type of skill set, but he does. That's where he is better than he was advertised.

"He just knows how to rebound and block shots with that slender body and not foul and still keep the ball in play. No one dominates like this kid does defensively."

Pratt says Davis in some ways reminds him of Artis Gilmore, Bill Walton and Akeem Olajuwon, all former NBA stars known for their defensive prowess.

"He's also like Cedric Maxwell that I coached at [North Carolina] Charlotte. Cedric had those long arms and blocked shots and kept the ball in play. They have similar skill sets," Pratt said. "Sam Bowie and Pervis Ellison also had long arms and could block shots and keep the ball inbounds.

"I am not saying who is better, but they all had similar body styles, weights. They all could block shots and stayed out of foul trouble like this kid does. But Davis is special, probably even more special than I even realized after I first saw him. You can't really appreciate him until you watch him play and see what he does over and over and over to impact games. We all thought he would be good, just not this good." ∎

Anthony Davis dives for a loose ball during Kentucky's January 14 win over Tennessee. (Victoria Graff)

SEC Tournament Quarterfinals

Game Date: March 9, 2012

Location: New Orleans, Louisiana

Score: Kentucky 60, LSU 51

Terrence Jones Plays Like He Deserves New Orleans Billboard, Too

By Larry Vaught

In order to help promote Anthony Davis as player of the year, the University of Kentucky paid for a huge billboard close to the Superdome with the same picture on it that was on a souvenir poster UK passed out earlier this season.

However, Friday it was Terrence Jones playing like he belonged on a billboard when No. 1 UK desperately needed someone to ignite the team against LSU in what was supposed to be a routine Southeastern Conference Tournament opening game for Kentucky. Instead, the Wildcats trailed 35–30 early in the second half before Jones scored nine straight points that helped lead to a 60–51 victory.

"In the second half, we just had to play more aggressive and play through the bumps and stuff," said Jones, who finished the game with 15 points, 11 rebounds, two steals and one blocked shot. "Coach challenged us at halftime to play tougher and drive more aggressively and make plays."

Jones did.

Terrence Jones brings the ball upcourt during Kentucky's win over LSU. Jones led a 9–0 run early in the second half to help Kentucky erase a five-point deficit. (Victoria Graff)

First, he scored off a lob from Darius Miller. Next he finished a drive. He was fouled on another drive and made one free throw. He hustled down the court to put in a Miller miss on a fast break. His lob to Anthony Davis for a score was negated when he was called for a charge, but he converted two free throws off a steal to give UK a 39–35 lead with his 9–0 spurt in a four-minute span.

"I was just trying to win," Jones said. "LSU was aggressive and really attacked us and went after steals. The second half we had to run our plays and be aggressive. That's what it takes in tournament play."

It does and Kentucky never surrendered the lead again in a game that freshmen Anthony Davis, Marquis Teague and Kyle Wiltjer all had some lapses while Michael Kidd-Gilchrist once again rose to the occasion with 19 points, nine rebounds, one steal, one block and one assist.

Davis finished with 12 points, 14 rebounds and six blocks, but he got his second foul midway of the first half and played only 13 minutes when UK struggled to lead 25–24 at intermission. Davis also had all four of his turnovers in the first half.

Teague admitted he was frustrated by his play, something that had not happened since December. He was 0-for-5 from the field and did not have a rebound. He finished with two points and five assists. "I've just got to be better. Coach Cal was not really on me that much other than telling me he knew I could do better," Teague said. "But I was frustrated with myself, something I tend to do and end up being too hard on myself."

Wiltjer played only seven minutes and did not take a shot or grab a rebound. He did block one shot, but he was not as physical as coach John Calipari wanted him to be.

"The freshmen can all learn just like I did last year," Jones, a sophomore, said. "We can't have another game where we come out lackadaisical or not ready to play like we did today."

Just ask senior Darius Miller, last year's SEC Tournament MVP. He was 0-for-2 from the field in only 17 minutes and had two rebounds, one assist and three of UK's 18 turnovers.

"LSU played hard and took advantage of us," Miller admitted. "At halftime I just told the guys we had to pick it up or go home. There's no excuse for the way we played."

But that's what is good about this team. It's rare, maybe impossible, for this talented team to have everyone play poorly at the same time and Jones — who had 27 points and nine rebounds in UK's 74–50 win at LSU — got the points UK needed most to make sure it won this game and continue its quest to be the overall No. 1 seed in the NCAA tourney.

"I felt when they played us early in the year, if he's going to play like that, they might as well crown them now because it is going to take a really, really good basketball team on a good day to beat this group," LSU coach Trent Johnson said. "Think about it. He was a preseason [SEC] player of the year. And he was one of the best freshmen in the conference and the country last year, and he either made first or second team [All-American]. So that speaks volumes to the quality of the league and to the quality of teams in our league."

Jones, who is UK's third leading scorer behind Davis and Doron Lamb, didn't surprise his teammates with what he did in this game.

"He just wanted the ball and made that clear," Lamb, who had 12 points, said. "He was calling for it. He was rebounding. He was pushing the ball up the court in transition. He played great, the way we know he can play. He's a big part of this team and we need him to do this in tournament play. He has been playing great the last couple of games and we expect him to keep doing that."

"He's a great player. When he's successful like that, we are just going to be that much more successful," Davis said.

Jones was quick to share credit with teammates, though. He wanted no part of the star role in this win.

"We just wanted to go to the post and get buckets inside," Jones said. "We were just running that play for me but we had the option to go to Mike [Kidd-Gilchrist]. They just started playing Mike because he was getting it going earlier in the first half, so it just made me more open in the second half and when that happens, I should score." ▪

Terrence Jones puts up a shot against LSU. Jones scored 15 points and grabbed 11 rebounds in the SEC Tournament win. (Victoria Graff)

SEC Tournament Semifinals

Game Date: March 10, 2012

Location: New Orleans, Louisiana

Score: Kentucky 74, Florida 71

Teague Heeds Calipari's Advice, Delivers on Promise to Play Better to Help Cats Beat Florida

By Larry Vaught

Marquis Teague felt like he let his Kentucky teammates down in Friday's 60–51 win over LSU and told them he would play better Saturday against Florida in the Southeastern Conference Tournament semifinals.

The freshman point guard even went to UK coach John Calipari's room Friday night and Calipari could sense the frustration Teague felt. He simply told him to be aggressive, drive inside and run the team.

Teague did all that — and made two free throws with 14.5 seconds to play to ice the game — in the 74–71 win over Florida that puts Kentucky into Sunday's tourney championship game for a third straight year under Calipari. Teague had 15 points, five assists, three rebounds and one steal. He was 6-for-9 from the field compared to 0-for-5 Friday when he had only two points and four turnovers.

"I just felt like I let our team down Friday. I had to play hard and aggressive for them and be a leader," said Teague, one of five Wildcats in double figures. "We feel like we are supposed to win every game we play. We are going to take a team's best shot and then we have to fire back."

Kentucky fired back in this game with a 14–0 run that turned a 56–51 deficit into a 65–56 lead with 6 minutes, 59 seconds to play. Sophomore Terrence Jones was the catalyst with seven of his 15 points in the run along with four rebounds, two steals and one assist. However, UK let Florida cut the deficit to 65–63 with 2:40 to play and went over five minutes

Doron Lamb lays the ball up during Kentucky's SEC Tournament semifinal win over Florida. Lamb scored 16 points. (Victoria Graff)

without a field goal. Jones hit two free throws with 34.6 seconds left to make it 70–66 and then Teague knocked down two with 14.5 seconds left for a 72–68 lead.

Teague, an Indiana native, missed a late free throw at Indiana in December that helped the Hoosiers rally to give UK its only loss. That memory was not on his mind.

"No, I didn't even think about that," he said. "I just knew we needed me to make the shots. I told them I was going to knock them down. I wanted to step up to the line and knock them in. I wanted to seal the win. I was confident."

Just like he knew when he got a chance he had to power his way inside the lane to finish shots or take open 15-foot jump shots in tempo that he can make and did make.

"That's my man. That's the Marquis Teague I know," freshman Michael Kidd-Gilchrist said. "Today he was just playing his game like he said he would. That's the Marquis we need and know."

Senior Darius Miller, who struggled through a second straight scoreless game for the first time this season, predicted after Friday's game that Teague would be fine.

"I said yesterday not to worry about him," Miller said. "He competes. I knew yesterday's game would drive him to play well and it did. I just know the player he is. He is a fierce competitor and has a huge drive to succeed. He is just that way."

Jones has been UK's best player in the first two games here and barely missed a second straight double-double — 15 points, nine rebounds, one steal, one assist. Like Miller, he was confident in UK's point guard to get rolling again.

"That's the type person and player he is. He felt they did not respect his game Friday and today he was much more aggressive," Jones said. "He drove and finished. He helped us get the win, but it's not like the first time he's done that. He's been good all year."

Kentucky had to rely on its balance to win a game that was much more difficult than either regular-season win over the Gators. Florida was 12-for-49 from 3-point range in the two regular-season losses to Kentucky. In this game, Florida was 11-for-22 while UK was only 5-for-17. That's an 18-point advantage.

"They were making a lot of 3's. That way my fault," Kidd-Gilchrist said. "I am blaming myself. [Bradley] Beal got really hot. He's a good player, but I have to do better."

Beal, who was recruited by Kentucky, had 20 points and was 4-for-7 from 3-point range. Erik Murphy was 4-for-4 from 3-point range and had 24 points because he often beat Jones and Anthony Davis down the court for easier shots than he got against Kentucky before.

"They only played six guys, we had our big emphasis on running the floor and getting out and score and push it out in transition," Florida center Patric Young said. "And it started wearing guys out a lot because we don't think they're in the best of shape."

Ouch.

That quote certainly will find its way into the UK locker room, but it did look that way. Maybe it's because most teams have tried to slow down Kentucky and the Cats have learned how to grind out wins more than how to outrun opponents.

"The tempo was fast," Davis, who had 15 points, 12 rebounds and two blocks, said. "They really tried to get up and down the floor. It was a fun game for both teams, a game we don't get to play that much."

That's what made it imperative for Teague to play well setting the table for UK's offense, and he did.

"I told him [Friday] that you can't play to score because that hurts our team," Calipari said. "You have to pick your spots and score in transition lay-ups. To keep them honest, if they don't play you, shoot foul shots. Drive it right there, pull up and shoot it. I got no problem.

"But you got a team that you need to get involved. And it's hard. It's hard playing point guard for us. I told the team, he was outstanding. The other guys when they get the ball, they're trying to put it in the basket. He's got to run us, he's got to call the offense and again, he's a freshman. He's got a toughness to him. I felt very comfortable with him going to that foul line."

As well as running UK's offense as efficiently as he did. ▪

Michael Kidd-Gilchrist (left) and Darius Miller celebrate as Kentucky advanced to the SEC Tournament final. (Victoria Graff)

SEC Tournament Title Game

Game Date: March 11, 2012

Location: New Orleans, Louisiana

Score: Kentucky 64, Vanderbilt 71

Cats Just Have to Learn from SEC Tourney Play and They Will Be Fine in NCAA

By Larry Vaught

Not a single Kentucky player bought into the theory that losing a game would help the team going into NCAA Tournament play. If anything, the players wanted to show that their "will to win" could put together a 31-game win streak.

However, Sunday's 71–64 loss to Vanderbilt in the Southeastern Conference Tournament title game does more damage to UK's ego/pride than its national championship hopes.

Syracuse, Kansas and North Carolina all lost in conference title games, too. It happens to teams and now Kentucky's challenge is to learn from what happened in the SEC tourney. LSU was more physical before UK rallied to win. Florida was faster in transition and hot from 3-point range before Kentucky rallied to win. But Sunday it was UK failing to get a field goal in the final eight minutes after taking a 59–55 lead. The Cats missed shot after shot against Vanderbilt's zone to end the game. Didn't matter if the Cats got inside the lane or fired away from 3-point range. The shots were off.

Vanderbilt made the Cats pay for having Michael Kidd-Gilchrist in foul trouble and for settling for too many 3-point tries (28). Vanderbilt made UK pay for defensive lapses.

Just like the two previous games, the Cats were not hitting on all cylinders. This time Darius Miller was superb — 16 points, four assists, three rebounds, two steals and one block

Freshman forward Kyle Wiltjer takes a shot during the SEC Tournament final. Wiltjer scored eight points in 11 minutes. (Victoria Graff)

— and Kyle Wiltjer gave some needed relief on both ends off the bench. However, Anthony Davis took too many 3-pointers, Terrence Jones — who still had a double-double with 12 points and 11 rebounds — had a long stretch where he was a non-factor and Doron Lamb was not the offensive player he must be for UK to win the national title.

Kentucky did not shoot well from 3-point range in the tournament and did not play its normal lock-down defense for 40 minutes in any game in New Orleans.

Yet the Cats beat Florida, a NCAA team, and Vandy had to play probably its best game of the year to beat Kentucky and possibly help its seeding in the NCAA.

But Kentucky is still capable of winning the national title. Davis had another double-double on an "off game" for him on his 19th birthday. Jones overall was superb in the tourney. Lamb won't go through a prolonged shooting slump. Miller got his game back together just as Marquis Teague did Saturday and Wiltjer should have gained confidence Sunday. And Kidd-Gilchrist, his intensity never changes.

The Cats should still be a No. 1 seed when NCAA pairings are announced at 6 p.m. and should open NCAA play in Louisville in front of another pro-UK crowd. Whether UK is placed in the St. Louis or Atlanta regional doesn't matter. Kentucky should win two games to advance and either place will be full of Kentucky fans.

The Wildcats just have to regain their swagger, re-focus on defense and get back to the offensive flow that made them so good all year. If they do that, Kentucky will be just fine for the rest of March. ■

Opposite: Doron Lamb shoots a 3-pointer against Vanderbilt. Lamb went 1-for-7 from behind the arc. Above: Michael Kidd-Gilchrist dunks the ball. The freshman forward played just 16 minutes in the loss. (Victoria Graff)

NCAA Tournament Second Round

Game Date: March 15, 2012

Location: Louisville, Kentucky

Score: Kentucky 81, Western Kentucky 66

Cats Know They Must Play Better, But Poor 3-Point Shooting Not a Big Worry to UK

By Larry Vaught

On a scale of one to 10, freshman Michael Kidd-Gilchrist — who is always blunt honest — only gave Kentucky about an eight for the way it played in Thursday's 81–66 win over Western Kentucky.

If the Cats want to keep advancing in the NCAA Tournament, Kidd-Gilchrist and his teammates have to do better, and they know it.

"Last year we got better every game in the NCAA Tournament and made the Final Four," said UK senior Darius Miller. "That's what we have to do again. You can't stay the same in this tournament or you get beat. You have to play better every game."

When will that happen, especially after UK was less than its best in the Southeastern Conference Tournament to end the season?

"Real soon," Kidd-Gilchrist said. "There's more to come. We've got to play with more confidence on offense and defense. I am going to get going more and I support all my teammates and know they will too."

Even Western coach Ray Harper, who knew his team was overmatched, knew the way Kentucky played in this game would not lead to an eighth national championship for the Wildcats.

"If they want to advance and win a national championship, they're going to have to shoot the ball better from the perimeter," Harper said. "Doron Lamb may have been the only one. Terrence [Jones] made a 3. They're going to have to find somebody else that can

Terrence Jones slams home two during the first half against Western Kentucky. Jones led the Cats with 22 points and 10 rebounds. (Clay Jackson)

make a shot from the perimeter. They're talented. They're extremely talented."

They are, but UK was 3-for-10 from 3-point range after going 1-for-8, 5-for-17 and 6-for-28 in the SEC tourney. That's 15-for-63 for 24 percent, not exactly a national championship number.

"We don't live and die by the 3," Miller said. "We don't need to focus on that. That's not what we do best. We have a lot of athletic player and try to finish more at the rim than we do shoot 3's."

Still, Miller is 2-for-14 in the last five games. Kidd-Gilchrist has made just one of his last 14 3-pointers in the last 17 games after going 11-for-32 to start the season. Marquis Teague is 0-for-4 from 3-point range the last four games. Terrence Jones is 3-for-9 in the last four games. Even Lamb, who was 2-for-4 Thursday, was only 5-for-18 in the previous four games coming into the tournament.

"I just come to play. I don't even care about stuff like that," Kidd-Gilchrist said. "I just have fun and don't want to lose. I just shoot when the shots are there."

Kentucky coach John Calipari did his best to downplay any worries about the recent poor shooting from his team.

"It's dangerous, if you come into a game and say we're almost a 40 percent 3-point shooting team. We just don't shoot that many because we don't need to. But if you give them to us, we'll shoot 20," Calipari said. "It's dangerous because all of a sudden, we make four, five in a row, you're down 16, 17, and it's hard in this tournament to do that. But there are games we shoot it better than others.

"One game we made — am I saying this right? — 15 threes I think we did. And there's another game we made one. On the season as a whole, we're almost a 40 percent 3-point shooting team. So it's dangerous to play a zone. It's dangerous to. You can do it, but what you're doing is let's hope they don't make shots today. That's a tough way to play."

One way Kentucky hopes to offset poor 3-point shooting is by playing faster like it did against Western. While Calipari said he emphasized defense to his team, the players talked about him urging them to run more.

"When we get out and run, we get easier looks and baskets," Anthony Davis said. "We are a fast-break team. We want to get back to Kentucky basketball that way."

But most importantly for Calipari, he's trying not to put any pressure on his team because others are doing that for him by talking and writing about how this is Kentucky's tournament to lose.

"Look, I've got a good team, and I've got good players. Let's worry about us playing as well as we can play. If that's not good enough, then it's done," Calipari said. "But that's what our challenge is, and that's what our goal is. Let's just play as well as we can play.

"Today, I talked to them prior to the game. Let's just worry about defense. I don't even care about offense. Let's just be a great defensive team today, and let's show everybody how we guard. I thought they did that in the first half, and they were fine until I went zone as a coach, and I wanted us to work on it a little bit in case we have to go to it."

His players don't seem worried.

"Whatever happens happens. We just play and have fun with it," Kidd-Gilchrist said. "It's the NCAA, something we have all dreamed about. We just know to play our best and see what happens. Shooting. Defense. Rebounding. Whatever. It's only about one thing, and that's winning." ■

Terrence Jones takes two Western Kentucky defenders with him to the basket during the first half. (Clay Jackson)

NCAA Tournament Third Round

Game Date: March 17, 2012

Location: Louisville, Kentucky

Score: Kentucky 87, Iowa State 71

Darius Miller Clutch Again in Wildcats' Win Over Iowa State

By Larry Vaught

Darius Miller knows it's crunch time. The Kentucky senior guard pounded his chest after connecting on a 3-pointer that proved be a momentum-changer in the second half of an 87–71 victory over Iowa State in the third round of the NCAA Tournament Saturday night at the KFC Yum! Center.

"We all came out with a lot of intensity," Miller said. "[We] were really focused on what we needed to do. We all know this is the last time this team is going to be together. We're not quite ready for that yet."

The trey by Miller was part of a 14–0 scoring blitz by the Wildcats that propelled his squad to the blowout win over the Cyclones. Miller finished with 19 points and had eight of those during the decisive spurt that sent the Wildcats (34–2) into the Sweet 16 for the third straight season and a rematch with Indiana, the only team that defeated Kentucky during the regular season 73–72 on Dec. 10 in Bloomington, Ind.

Miller was emotional during the second half against the Cyclones, nodding his head and clapped his hands after popping a three-pointer with 10 minutes remaining. He wasn't ready to hang up his sneakers for the final time in his collegiate career.

Anthony Davis dunks during the first half of Kentucky's win over Iowa State. Davis scored 19 points. (Clay Jackson)

"We all were emotional," Miller said. "We showed a lot of emotion, played with a lot of intensity and had a lot of fun with it all. It's coming to an end and hopefully we can continue and go get a championship."

Miller made three of Kentucky's 10 shots from long range, many of which came at critical times during the contest.

"He was hyped," said Kentucky guard Marquis Teague. "He knocked down big shots when we needed them. He was on fire tonight. We were all into the game and nobody wanted to lose. We knew this was a good team, so we had to come out fired up."

After scoring just six points in an 81–66 victory over Western Kentucky Thursday, Miller eclipsed that total in the first half against the Cyclones. Miller came off the bench and scored seven points and had five of those during a brief 10–0 run by the Wildcats, turning a 13–11 advantage into a 23–11 lead.

The Kentucky senior connected on a pair of 3-pointers during the spurt, but one was waved off and changed to a deuce following a review by the officials. The Kentucky senior added a pair of assists and a block during the opening half.

In the second half, Miller was just as effective. He scored 12 points and provided much-needed leadership for the rest of his teammates against an Iowa State team that provided a physical test for the Wildcats going into Friday night's rematch against the Hoosiers.

"We know basketball is a game of runs and they're a good team," he said. "They did a great job of coming back, but we had a run, too."

Now that the team's attention has shifted from Iowa State to Indiana, Miller is taking a low-key approach to the contest and isn't getting into the hype surrounding the rematch.

"I'm just as excited [about the game] as I was today," he said. "It's our next game and we can't take it as a revenge game or anything like that. We've got to take it like it's our last game, because if we lose, that's it. They beat us before, so we know they're capable of beating us and we've got to come out ready to go. We're a totally different team and I know they are too and we've got to come out ready to play."

Like the rest of his teammates, Miller is looking forward to a return to the Georgia Dome, where he was named the Most Valuable Player in last year's Southeastern Conference Tournament. This time, the stakes will be higher for the Cats. ■

Opposite: Marquis Teague shoots over Iowa State's Bubu Palo during the first half. Teague led Kentucky with 24 points and added seven assists. Above: Coach John Calipari reacts during Kentucky's win over Iowa State. (Clay Jackson)

NCAA Tournament Sweet 16

Game Date: March 23, 2012

Location: Atlanta, Georgia

Score: Kentucky 102, Indiana 90

Cats Feel Right at Home in Georgia Dome in Win Over Indiana

By Keith Taylor

Revenge was sweet for Kentucky. The Wildcats erased the pain of a buzzer-beating, one-point loss to Indiana earlier this year with a 102–90 victory over the Hoosiers in the NCAA South Region semifinals this morning at the Georgia Dome. It ended more than three months of frustration for the Wildcats, who swore revenge wasn't a factor earlier this week despite the pregame hype surrounding the much-anticipated rematch.

It was hard to notice Kentucky wasn't thinking about its previous experience against Indiana. Even Kentucky coach John Calipari denied the notion that avenging December's 73–72 loss was the motivating factor behind his team's performance in front of a Georgia Dome crowd that resembled a louder version of the team's Big Blue contingent at Rupp Arena.

By the final buzzer, they were loud and proud in a city known as "Catlanta" all throughout Big Blue Nation. Kentucky has fared well in the Peach State and the successful trend continued against the Hoosiers when it mattered the most even under adversity.

Michael Kidd-Gilchrist led Kentucky with 24 points as the Wildcats avenged their only regular-season loss, defeating Indiana to advance to the Elite 8. (Clay Jackson)

"It was a war," Kentucky coach John Calipari said afterward. "Indiana played great and we just played a little bit better."

The last time Kentucky visited Atlanta, the Wildcats left town with the Southeastern Conference Tournament trophy in hand, sparking a memorable postseason run that propelled Kentucky to last year's Final Four in Houston.

Although the final margin was by double figures, getting there wasn't an easy task for the overall top-seeded Wildcats.

Kentucky center Anthony Davis sat and watched the final 14 minutes of the opening half after picking up two fouls in the first six minutes. For the first time in the Big Dance, Davis was forced to be a spectator instead of a contributor.

While on the bench, Davis got a sideline view of Christian Watford, the Hoosier Superhero who drained the game-winner in the Hoosiers' last-second heroics in Bloomington. Watford tallied 17 points and even got up a 3-pointer to end the half, but this time it wasn't similar to the one that resulted in Kentucky's one-point setback that was the team's only blemish prior to the postseason. Watford's production was limited in the second half and Kentucky held him to just 10 points.

Despite the absence of Davis and Watford's hot hand, Kentucky held its own and led 50–47 at the break, with Terrence Jones and Michael Kidd-Gilchrist combining for 23 points. Jones scored just four points in the first meeting between the two border rivals, but had 12 points in a game that had more meaning and bigger

Opposite: Anthony Davis blocks a Cody Zeller shot in the second half. Above: Marquis Teague dunks the ball in the first half for two of his 14 points on the night. (Clay Jackson)

stakes with a trip to the South Region final hanging in the balance.

"My teammates just told me to come out and play hard and score the ball," Davis said.

Calipari said Davis returned to his usual self in the second half and wasn't surprised by his performance that made it even more difficult on the Hoosiers, especially in the paint.

"He played like he always does," Calipari said. "I've never seen him play a bad game. He's a great player."

Davis was on the floor consistently in the final half and finished with nine points, 12 rebounds and three blocked shots, despite playing just 25 minutes. Even without Davis at full force, Kentucky created spacing between the two teams down the stretch and reached the century mark.

"That was a hard-fought battle," Indiana coach Tom Crean said. "No one really got momentum."

Kentucky got just enough to claim redemption. ◾

Opposite: Michael Kidd-Gilchrist goes up for two in the first half. Above: Terrence Jones grabs a rebound. (Clay Jackson)

Hoosiers Score 90 Points, but Crean Still Praises Kentucky's "Really Good Defense"

By Larry Vaught

Indiana coach Tom Crean was at a loss after Friday's 102–90 defeat by Kentucky to explain what might be the best way to attack Kentucky and win.

"We scored 90 points. We scored 90 points. They're a really good team. They've got a lot of guys. They've got a guy coming off the bench that's going to be a first round draft pick in Darius Miller. They're tremendous," Crean said.

"So I don't know if I can break down the game based on this game. We did a lot of good things, but they're a very talented team. As I said many times, I think it's obvious, they're extremely well coached. He is a great coach. It's one thing to have talent; it's a whole other thing to get them to be as good as they are defensively.

"This game came down to, when we had the ball moving, and offensively, when we could create some movement and get them off team defense, then we had some opportunities. But that's a lot easier said than done. Their defense, as good as they are offensively and as talented as they are, the strength of their team is their defense. And we did some good things tonight, but at the same time, that defense is really, really good." ■

Darius Miller drives to the basket during Kentucky's Sweet 16 win over Indiana. (Clay Jackson)

NCAA Tournament Elite Eight

Game Date: March 25, 2012

Location: Atlanta, Georgia

Score: Kentucky 82, Baylor 70

Terrence Jones Shows He Can Impact Kentucky by Doing More Than Just Scoring

By Larry Vaught

There was a time when Terrence Jones felt he had to score to impact games. He can still do that, but now the Kentucky sophomore can also do much more to change a game.

He proved that Sunday during Kentucky's 82–70 win over Baylor that sends Jones and UK to a second straight Final Four.

In the first half, he had one point and took only two shots. But, and it is a big but, he had five defensive rebounds, three blocked shots and two steals. He was UK's best defensive player and played perhaps the best defensive half of his UK career.

On offense, he was just as important without scoring because he has six assists — one more than his career high. They all came in the first 14 minutes when UK used a dazzling 31–5 run to build a 36–17 lead that all but assured there would be a Kentucky-Louisville rematch in the national semifinals.

"I was just trying to be aggressive," said Jones. "Once I went to the hole, Anthony [Davis] was so wide open. I was just basically throwing lobs to him. It was a real physical battle and I had to really play hard and aggressive and that led to great rebounding position that I could start the break with."

In the second half, UK needed more offense from Jones and he responded with 11 points. He was 3-for-5 from the field and would have had more points if he had not gone 5-for-10 from the foul line.

Anthony Davis (left) and Michael Kidd-Gilchrist celebrate as Kentucky topped Baylor to advance to the Final Four. (Clay Jackson)

Still, he had 12 points, nine rebounds, six assists, three blocks and two steals in 35 minutes to more than offset his two turnovers.

Just call it Redemption Weekend for Jones. He had 12 points, five rebounds, one block and one steal against Indiana Friday to help wipe out memories of his miserable performance in UK's loss at Indiana.

Now he's Final Four-bound again and close to achieving his goal of winning a national title, the reason he came back to Kentucky rather than leave for the NBA like teammates Brandon Knight and DeAndre Liggins did after the 2011 Final Four run.

"Well, it feels great [to go back to the Final Four]. Just working so hard all year with this group and us just coming together to become a family and just celebrating getting this far is just real good. We just know we've got a lot more to do," Jones said.

Indeed there is, especially with rival Louisville waiting for Kentucky in New Orleans in what could be the biggest basketball game ever for both teams. Win this game and own the state. Lose this game and it's unthinkable, or at least it is for Kentucky since the Cats already have one win over Louisville and have been favored to win the title all season. Not winning the national title because of a loss to the Cards would be Big Blue misery.

"We are not going to add that pressure on ourselves," Jones said. "We are going to stay with our same routine."

Can the Cats really avoid the Final Four/Louisville hype?

"On this team, yes. We have a bunch of fun loving dudes," Jones said. "We'll be fine."

Maybe better than fine when Jones is locking down on defense the way he did, distributing the ball, rebounding and starting the fast break.

"He was great," freshman Michael Kidd-Gilchrist, who was named the South Region's most outstanding player, said. "He was doing everything, but we know he can do that. It was no big surprise. Whatever we need, Terrence does it. That's nothing new."

Maybe, but the way Jones did it Sunday was a bit different because he was so unselfish and so determined. He had that intense look on his face that he would not be denied.

"I am definitely happy when my teammates score more and all I have to do is pass to them," Jones said. "I just want to win. That's it. We have that will to win. We have had it all season. We just lock down on people and take pride in what we do. We're happy we won, but we know there's more to do. That's why we can't make too big a deal out of this. It was a great win, but there's more to do."

Kentucky players openly admit that anything less than a national championship and they will consider this year where they went unbeaten in Southeastern Conference regular season play, have won 35 games and have been ranked No. 1 most of the season a disappointment. Some might consider that unrealistic. Jones considers it logical.

"This is a great team. We are a family. I love my brothers and we have great players," Jones said. "Everybody wants to win a national championship. That's why we are here. We don't want to settle for anything less than that. So if we don't win, we'll be disappointed. How could we not be?"

That's setting a high bar for a successful season, but that's part of playing at Kentucky and Jones played like he truly understood every bit of that and that's why UK is now so close to reaching that lofty expectation. ▪

Michael Kidd-Gilchrist drives to the basket as Terrence Jones looks on. Kidd-Gilchrist led Kentucky with 19 points. (Clay Jackson)

Darius Miller Savors Return to Final Four

By Keith Taylor

Darius Miller isn't thinking about Louisville. He's stuck in the moment.

The Kentucky senior is savoring the Wildcats' 82–70 victory over Baylor in the South Region finals Sunday afternoon at the Georgia Dome. Although it would be easy for Miller to look ahead to Saturday's national semifinal against instate rival Louisville, he's not buying into the hype, at least for now. He doesn't plan on thinking about the Cardinals until at least Tuesday.

"This feels good and we're all taking it in, especially the younger guys," Miller said. "We could care less about who we play [Saturday]. When we start preparation, that's when we'll start focusing on what we need to do."

The feeling, Miller said, resembles last year's 76–69 victory over North Carolina in the East Region title in Newark, N.J.

"It feels the same — it's a great feeling and I'm happy to be a part of something like this," he said. "I'm happy to have the amount of support with the teams [I've been on] here at Kentucky."

Although the Wildcats lost to eventual National Champion Connecticut 56–55 in the national semifinals last year, Miller hasn't forgotten last year's trek to the Final Four at Reliant Stadium in Houston.

"It's something you'll never forget," he said. "All of the teams in college work hard to get to this point and we're here right now. We're blessed to be here and we're ready to take today and [Monday] to enjoy it."

Reminiscent of his previous performances in the Georgia Dome, Miller scored eight points against the Bears and drained a jumper during a monstrous 31–5 run by Kentucky. The blitz carried the Cats throughout the remainder of the contest.

"We knew they weren't going to go away easy," Miller said. "We just tried to keep playing the way we wanted to play [and] keep our energy up."

The senior guard tallied 19 points in a 102–90 victory over Indiana in the regional semifinals Friday night. In his team's four-game run in the NCAA Tournament, Miller is averaging 17 points per game. Along with his contributions, Miller has been getting help from his teammates, especially Michael Kidd-Gilchrist, named the Most Outstanding Player in the South Region. The players want to win a national title for Miller.

"I have a lot of respect for them and they have a lot of respect for me," he said. "I really care for them and they care for me. We're like brothers at this point. We've got a lot of love for each other and I want to win a [national title] for them too."

Once he arrives back in Lexington, Miller knows the attention will shift to the Cardinals.

"At this point, we're just trying to enjoy being [in the Final Four]," he said.

Following Louisville's 72–68 triumph over Florida in the West Regional finals, the Cardinals wanted an opportunity for a rematch with the Wildcats in on a neutral court. Miller said the chatter "means nothing" at this moment in time.

"I'm just trying to enjoy going to the Final Four right now," he said. "We'll be prepared when we start preparation. I know we're going to do all we can to be prepared for them. It's going to be a good game."

Although Louisville is in the back of his mind. He knows the hype surrounding the contest is "going to be crazy."

"We already for that," he said. "It's crazy for a regular-season game. We know how it's going to be." ■

Darius Miller cuts down the net after Kentucky defeated Baylor to advance to the Final Four. (Clay Jackson)

Clay Jackson